AU SABLE
POINT
LIGHTHOUSE

AU SABLE POINT LIGHTHOUSE

BEACON ON LAKE SUPERIOR'S SHIPWRECK COAST

MIKEL B. CLASSEN

Charleston   London

THE
History
PRESS

Published by The History Press
Charleston, SC 29403
www.historypress.net

Copyright © 2014 by Mikel B. Classen
All rights reserved

First published 2014

Manufactured in the United States

ISBN 978.1.62619.483.0

Library of Congress CIP data applied for.

To my dad, Harry J. Classen. He would have really liked this.

CONTENTS

ACKNOWLEDGEMENTS

S pecial thanks to Jack Deo of Superior View Studio of Marquette and Brenda St. Martins from the National Park Service at Pictured Rocks National Lakeshore for all their help securing historical photographs for this project. I would also like to thank Mary L. Underwood for chauffeuring, catering, input, assistance and support throughout this project. It couldn't have been done without her.

INTRODUCTION

A few years back, I moved to a small town along the Lake Superior shoreline in Michigan called Grand Marais. I was very excited about this because Grand Marais was located at the eastern end of a national park called Pictured Rocks National Lakeshore. I had explored much of Michigan's Upper Peninsula as a feature writer, but I hadn't had the opportunity to spend any real quality time in the National Lakeshore. Now I would have the chance to get to know it intimately, which I wasted no time in doing.

Because it was nearby, Au Sable Point became one of the places I frequently visited. First it was the Hurricane River that attracted me because my father had told me about it. It was one of his favorite places to fish. He used to drive four hundred miles to get there, so I figured it had to be something special.

I had learned there was a lighthouse to the east at Au Sable Point, and I followed the trail to get there. It was unmarked along the road coming in, so someone going to the Hurricane had to know about it to get out there. The national park wasn't trying to get visitors to the lighthouse yet. When I arrived out there, they were beginning the restoration of the assistant keeper's duplex. There was a park ranger working at the light, so I decided to find out what I could about the old light station. He (I wish I could remember his name) was delighted in this and offered to give me a tour of the lighthouse, including taking me up into the light tower. He was a fountain of information.

We went into the duplex, and he showed me what they were doing and explained all of the trim and woodwork they had to replace. He was very proud, and I was thrilled that he was spending the time to talk to me. He took me into the basement and showed me the old oil barrels. Then he took me around the grounds and explained the purpose of each and every building.

As we were walking, he mentioned he'd been looking for the lighthouse dump but hadn't found it yet. Looking around, I pointed down into a low hollow off to the edge of the clearing that surrounded the lighthouse. "My guess would be over there," I told him. "That's where I would have put it." We took a walk over and kicked through the leaves. Sure enough, we started kicking loose some old kerosene cans that had been used to fuel the light. I felt rather pleased with myself.

That ranger piqued my interest in Au Sable Point, and the place has never left me. Nor has the memory of that day. I started collecting information and stories about the lighthouse, and I was able to get copies of the lighthouse logs from the national park. I made countless visits to Au Sable and watched the ongoing restoration over the years. I spent time photographing the lighthouse and Au Sable Point and camped there in the primitive tent sites for several nights. I got to know Au Sable well.

When standing at Au Sable, this seemingly benign section of shoreline is deceptive. Today, it is surrounded by quiet beaches and lush forests, much like it was in the past. But as a part of Pictured Rocks National Lakeshore, one of our finest national parks, there are a few more visitors making the walk to the station. It's not so alone anymore, but little else has changed. Breathtaking views of the colossal Grand Sable Sand Dunes can be found to the east toward Grand Marias. To the west are beaches that have freshwater springs seeping into the beach and Lake Superior. The Hurricane River teems with trout. My father once told me that the trout were so thick in the Hurricane that you could walk across it on their backs. I've never quite seen that, but it is full of fish.

The thick forest still stands in all its majesty, filling in the miles surrounding Au Sable and providing one of the finest glimpses of nature's wilderness. It's only when walking the shoreline that Au Sable's true nature hits home. The *Mary Jarecki*, the *Sitka* and the *Gale Staples* all lay still on the shore, and countless pieces of other wrecks are scattered between. No longer is Au Sable simply a beach; it is a graveyard, a watery cemetery where remnants of ships are the tombstones of the nameless lost. Au Sable Point is a place of paradox, yin and yang. What is admired today for its beauty and uniqueness was dreaded in the past, feared to the marrow—and the fear was justified.

Au Sable Point is a place of mystery and tragedy. Located on the southern shore of Lake Superior in the heart of the region known as the "Shipwreck Coast," Au Sable, called Big Sable in its early years, is a graveyard of ships and men that stands alone among the Great Lakes. It is an extraordinary place that attracted extraordinary events.

To this day, the shoreline is littered with the remains of the wrecks of the past. Skeletons of ships and debris testify to the past that has earned the point's reputation for danger and disaster. The lighthouse that was erected there as a warning for sailors who braved the violence of Lake Superior wasn't able to avert the loss of cargo, ships and lives that would cement Au Sable Point as a Great Lakes legend.

The wind shifts suddenly. What was once calm water is whipped into whitecaps, and the icy fingers of a north wind caress the face. The sky goes from blue to gray, and in a matter of minutes, all has changed. The waves build to three feet—then five. In the distance is the sound of a motor as a small fishing boat races to the safety of Grand Marais Harbor. The rollers build and pound. It's time to get under cover. It's about to get nasty.

CHAPTER 1
THE EARLY YEARS (BEFORE THE LIGHTHOUSE)

The origin of Au Sable Point begins with the glaciers. Around 10,000 BC, the glaciers began to recede from the face of North America. As the glaciers moved and thawed, they carved out the region that became Lake Superior and the other Great Lakes. When they melted, the water that was left behind made up the largest bodies of fresh water anywhere on Earth, and the glacial action had sculpted a landscape like no other.

The Lake Superior region was graced with cliffs of spectacular beauty and granite mountains that held precious minerals. Atop it all grew a wilderness of great pine and hardwoods. The region abounded with game and wildlife.

Lake Superior itself created a harshness of climate that was all its own. Violent storms, blinding blizzards and frigid temperatures were all products of the icy cold water that the lake held. When warm air moved across cold water, or when frigid air moved across warmer water, they combined to make the most dangerous storms. Michigan territorial governor Lewis Cass once stated, "There are four Great Lakes, and there's one that's Superior." Lake Superior was truly a unique place on earth.

Beneath the icy waters, the glaciers left behind a finger of sandstone that protruded a mile into Lake Superior, hidden but deadly. Its irregular shape caused it to rise as high as only six feet beneath the surface in some places. This reef would be named Au Sable. To the west of it were the great colored cliffs of Pictured Rocks. To the east were the towering Grand Sable Sand Dunes. At the heart were Au Sable Point and the sandstone reef. Nature had created an instrument of deadly destruction.

But nature wasn't through with Au Sable. In addition to the offshore reef, the area was infamous for thick fog caused by the interaction of cool lake air with the warmer air rising from nearby Grand Sable Dunes. The resulting fog could completely obscure the shoreline, hiding the landmarks used to navigate safely. Then there were the storms; huge gales accompanied by violent winds would assail the area. Because of its enormous depth, Lake Superior's water remains an icy cold temperature year-round, facilitating severe localized weather that is equipped with the utmost violence. Due to Lake Superior's breadth and prevailing north and west winds, the southern shore takes the worst beating the lake can muster. Hurricane-force winds accompanied by waves that can reach fifty feet have been recorded. There is nothing like a Lake Superior gale, and Au Sable Point gets hit with its full fury every time.

COASTING

The vessels that would eventually ply these waters were shallow draft boats powered by wind, steam or both. Equipped with only compasses and a sailor's "dead reckoning," ships' masters navigated by keeping land in sight. This method was fraught with problems in Lake Superior. First, compasses were unreliable. Large deposits of iron ore surrounded the lake, including deposits of magnetite. If a compass is anywhere near one of these, it will not register correctly. Second, Lake Superior fogs can be very dense, as can the cloud cover, and dead reckoning can't be used if the stars aren't visible.

The practice of sailing in view of the shore was referred to as "coasting" and was common for ships bound from or to Sault Ste. Marie and various points on Lake Superior. For steamers, both those with paddle wheels and propellers, frequent stops were necessary to pick up the cordwood needed to fire their boilers, necessitating the need for near-shore travel.

Coasting only added to the dangers of sailing Lake Superior. If the interplay of land and water produced intense fog along the coast, dangerous reefs and looming headlands could place a ship in jeopardy in a matter of moments, these being the hazards of sailing too close to the shoreline. Coasting also reduced a ship's maneuvering room. If a strong northerly blow came up, a ship under sail or steaming with an underpowered engine could be driven by wind and wave onto a shoal or beach, often resulting in the ship being battered to pieces.

With the combination of these factors, Au Sable Point was a natural ship trap, waiting to spring on unsuspecting and lost ships.

FUR TRADE

When the early French explorers arrived in Lake Superior looking for furs, they started an era of trade in the region. These voyageurs became regular visitors to Lake Superior. They plied the waters with their immense canoes, sixty-four feet in length, transporting tons of furs back to Montreal to be loaded onto ships for export back to France. This hardy breed of men could paddle more than 150 miles in a day.

One of those men, an early explorer named Pierre Espirit Radisson, made several trips into Lake Superior. He kept an extensive journal of his travels and commented about Au Sable. In 1622, Radisson noted that it was "most dangerous when there is any storms." With that pronouncement, Au Sable was recognized as a hazard to Lake Superior mariners. On the French maps, the area was noted as Aux Sable Pointe (the Sand Point). Radisson would camp there for the night at the mouth of a stream that would one day be known as Hurricane River.

The fur trade grew, and companies like the French Hudson Bay Company and the British Northwest Fur Company were established. The two competed hard (and sometimes violently) for control of the furs in the region, some conflicts resulting in massacres. When the French withdrew from North America in 1763, Canada came into British control. The Northwest Fur Company dominated the northern Great Lakes. That all changed when the British lost the American Revolution. The Great Lakes were split down the middle, giving the southern portions to America and the north shore to Britain, now Canada.

With the success of the American Revolution, American interest in the Lake Superior trade was inevitable. When the border was drawn, the line went north of Isle Royale and across to Grand Portage, essentially making most of the Lake Superior basin American territory.

John Jacob Astor's American Fur Company entered the region to compete with the Northwest Fur Company. Furs were a craze, and demand and profits were high. Astor's company built warehouses and facilities at Mackinac Island and Sault Ste. Marie. Trading posts were established to collect the furs from Native Americans and trappers all along the shores of the Great Lakes, including Lake Superior. The long canoes of the voyageurs were making regular cargo runs back and forth. The water-bound traffic was considerable.

But things would soon change. The demand for more and more furs was outgrowing the supply. The system of the voyageurs and the great canoes was slow, and cargo capacity was limited. As early as the late 1790s, the Northwest Fur Company began building small sailing ships on Lake Superior. We know little about these, as few records survive, but it is speculated that there may have been as few as five and as many as twelve. The capacity and speed of a small sailing ship would have been a great improvement and a logical evolution in reaching a more efficient method of transporting the furs. These ships would make a regular route in hitting the trading posts, dropping off supplies and returning with a ship full of furs. These early trading posts were located at Sault Ste. Marie, Grand Marais, La Pointe and Grand Portage.

Though the region had been explored by the French and British, the newly established United States knew very little about it other than rumors. There were tales of riches not just from furs but minerals as well. There were also strange stories of mountains of solid copper, and rumors of gold and silver followed along with them. From the American perspective, the region was unexplored. A closer look was required.

In 1820, an American expedition into the Lake Superior region was undertaken by Michigan territorial governor Lewis Cass. Going along on this expedition was a young geologist named Douglas Houghton, who would discover copper in the Keweenaw a few years later. The purpose of the expedition was to map the region and determine what it held. At the time, no American official had explored north of Mackinac. The aforementioned rumors had circulated for years, inspiring a curiosity in Governor Cass. At the time, the Michigan Territory reached all the way to the Mississippi River in modern-day Minnesota. It was a vast tract of land that Cass knew very little about. He had to rectify that, and so he organized his expedition.

Several members of the expedition, including the noted Henry Schoolcraft, eventual discoverer of the source of the Mississippi River, kept journals. Schoolcraft writes of Au Sable:

> On passing along the coast of the Grand Sable [Dunes], we observed, through the water which is very transparent, large tubular rocks at the bottom of the lake beneath our canoes, and on encamping a short distance west of the termination of these sand banks, at La Pointe La Grand Sable, we found apparently a similar rock, jutting out upon the shore of the lake and rising to an elevation of eight or ten feet above the water. On examination, this proved to be a variegated sandstone in horizontal strata, tolerably compact, and consisting of coarse grains of silicious sand. Its color is white or red and arranged in spots and stripes.

What Schoolcraft describes here is what has become known as "Jacobsville" sandstone. It is a hard and unforgiving shale, not soft and crumbling like some types of sandstone.

That evening, as they camped at Au Sable near the mouth of the creek, the fury of Superior was unleashed. Again, Schoolcraft writes:

> *We encamped on a beach of sand near the entrance of a small creek which, from a violent storm that raged during the night, was called Hurricane Creek* [it still bears that name]. *This storm had threatened us before reaching the land, and in a short time, the wind raged with the utmost violence, and threw the lake into such disorder that the water drove into the Governor's marquee, pitched fifty yards from the margin, and lashed it down. At the same time the thunder was very frequent and severe, and when the fury of the gale abated, a heavy rain drenched every part of our camp.*—*June 20, 1820*

Au Sable Point had left an impression with Schoolcraft and Governor Cass. It was an impression that Au Sable would give time and time again to many who crossed its path.

SHIPWRECKS BEGIN

As stated earlier, the Northwest Fur Company had built a small fleet of ships. Different sources vary on how many and how early they were built, but they were the first known sailing ships on Lake Superior. In 1829, a small wooden sloop schooner named the *Otter* was one of those ships. In a northwest gale, it hit Au Sable Point and sank with all hands offshore of Grand Sable Dunes. It was the beginning of what would be a continuing trend at Au Sable Point.

The 1840s saw the discovery of copper in the Keweenaw Peninsula and, not long after, iron ore in Marquette and Duluth. Migration to the region grew dramatically, as did traffic on Lake Superior. Sailing ships and side-wheelers carried raw materials to Sault Ste. Marie to be shipped to industrial centers to the south. Immigrants coming north grew from a trickle to a flood with the opening of the Soo Locks canal at Sault Ste. Marie in 1855.

Before the lock, ships and goods had to be portaged through the city to bypass the rapids of the St. Mary's River, which had been an obstacle even for the voyageurs. As sailing ships became necessary, they had to be built on Lake Superior and would have to sail there exclusively. If a ship had to go above or below the rapids, the entire ship would have to be pulled out of the water and rolled through the city of Sault Ste. Marie (using logs placed under the hull and pulled by ropes) until it was past the rapids.

It took two years to complete the Soo Locks project, which brought thousands of workers into Sault Ste. Marie. When the project was completed, all the workers were laid off, and the businesses that had thrived on transferring ships and cargo around the rapids were now obsolete and were forced to adjust or go bankrupt. Many of the laid-off men moved on to work the copper mines and iron mines that would be increasing their outputs due to the opening of the Soo Locks.

The construction of the locks changed everything for vessels on Lake Superior. Ships could now come and go freely, and access to the lower lakes from Superior was no longer a problem. Navigating Lake Superior became a priority of the maritime community, which quickly began to establish lighthouses.

A light at Whitefish Point had been established in 1849, and in 1856, a light was built on the north side of Grand Island off Munising. But there was no other light between these two stations, and the eighty miles that separated them had proven to be some of the most treacherous waters in all of the Great Lakes. The frequent loss of ships in this area earned it the name "Shipwreck Coast." At the center of it were Au Sable Point and its sandstone reef.

In the summer of 1858, a side-wheeler named the *Lady Elgin* ran aground on Au Sable reef. For two days, it stayed there stranded. The captain and crew waited, not knowing if they would sight a ship and be rescued before a storm rose. Finally, the ship was spotted by the steamer *Illinois*, which took on the *Lady Elgin*'s cargo and then pulled it free. The ship suffered only minor damage.

Four years later, in 1862, during one of the fogs the region was notorious for, disaster struck. The *Oriole*, a schooner carrying ore, collided with the steamer *Illinois* and was cut in half. Neither ship had seen the other, and the collision came as a complete surprise. All hands of the *Oriole* were lost except one. The disaster was the direct result of the Au Sable fog. The incident cast a light on the need for more navigational aids in the area, and the maritime community began putting pressure on the U.S. Lighthouse Board. In an 1867 annual report, the board requested a congressional appropriation of $40,000 for the construction of a new coast light at a point between the Grand Island and Whitefish Point lights. Congress ignored the request, but the board remained persistent for the next four years.

The *Oneida Chief* was the next victim of the Point. In May 1868, during a spring storm, the ship ran aground and broke in two. The waves were high and churning, and the crew barely made it to shore. The cargo of pig iron from Marquette went to the bottom. Eventually, a salvage crew stripped the *Oneida Chief* of usable parts and recovered most of the cargo. Only the ship's bones remain on the bottom of Lake Superior.

CHAPTER 2

THE LIGHTHOUSE

The situation was getting serious. Men were dying, and ships were sinking; something had to be done. Since changing Lake Superior's weather wasn't an option, it was time for something that was an option: a lighthouse. Other lighthouses had been springing up around Lake Superior—why not at Au Sable? The *Marquette Mining Journal*, in its July 29, 1871 edition, wrote, "In all navigation of Lake Superior, there is none more dreaded by the mariner than that from Whitefish Point to Grand Island."

The Eleventh Lighthouse District, which administered the region and its light stations, stated in its annual report of 1871 that "a light was more a necessity at Au Sable Point than at any other unprotected location in the district." In the shipping year of 1870–71 alone, Lake Superior had claimed 214 lives along the dreaded coast. It was the push that was needed. The following year, with the public, the district office and the Lighthouse Board applying pressure, Congress appropriated $40,000 for a lighthouse at Au Sable. It was a much-needed victory.

A site was selected, and the State of Michigan sold 326 acres of land to the federal government for $407. Eleventh Lighthouse District engineer Brevet Brigadier General Orlando M. Poe began work on a design for the new station. At the same time, a new light station at Outer Island in the Apostle Islands was also in the planning stages. Poe was in charge of designing that station as well. Poe realized that both stations were to perform essentially the same functions, so he decided that the same plan would work for both locations. Work began in 1873, and an announcement of the event was

Men died along the "Shipwreck Coast" with an alarming frequency. This 1860s woodcut by Thomas Moran, featured in many publications of the time, depicts the constant hazard of sailing along the Pictured Rocks shoreline. *Author's collection.*

published in the *Marquette Mining Journal* on July 19 of that year: "The U.S. Lighthouse steamer *Warrington* passed up with a gang of workmen to build a lighthouse at Sable Point, near Grand Marais." With that, the construction crew for Au Sable Point Lighthouse set sail.

Poe's design for Au Sable was very unique at the time. Up until then, government facilities had always been built using "shoebox" designs, which centered on functionality and not aesthetics. However, Poe thought his lighthouses could contain the beauty and grandeur of a stately home while maintaining the feel of a government facility. The previous years had shown that the austere living in the isolation of remote locations only added to the breakdown of many light keepers. Anything that could alleviate the stress needed to be done.

Poe realized that since the keepers and their families would have to live at these stations for extended periods, they needed to be comfortable and feel at home. With that in mind, he designed gables and arches on the roof of the residence. The tower was connected to the house with a walkway so that the keepers could be protected from the weather when walking between them. The residence would be a two-story house with an attic and a full basement. Poe used wrought iron extensively, adding artistic touches within the ironwork, including the ornate spiral staircase that led up to the tower room. Architecturally, Au Sable was magnificent.

Poe changed how lighthouses were perceived and designed. The Au Sable light, with its attached tower, wrought-iron features and tapering tower, was the first of many lighthouses to be built in Poe's signature style. He went on to design light stations all around the Great Lakes—at Seul Choix, Wind Point, Grosse Point, Outer Island (Au Sable's twin), Presque Isle on Lake Huron, South Manitou Island and Little Sable Point—all of which carry this signature look. His towers embodied grace and strength, while the keeper's quarters promoted

The iron staircase that spiraled up into the light tower was a work of art. This photo shows the detail of the ironwork. *Photo by Mikel B. Classen.*

comfort and space. It was all meant to make life for those who lived there the best it could be. The life at a light station was hard enough. Poe cared for his charges, the light keepers, and worked for their well-being.

Construction workers had cleared the area and set up a camp, a small tent city. They would have to stay there while the light station was built. Building supplies were shipped in, and a log dock was built to unload the boats. It was hot and buggy—workers were prey for the insects. In spite of it, the construction went along at a steady pace. The great tower was raised, its foundation anchored on solid bedrock twenty-three feet below the surface. The walls of the tower were over four feet thick at the base and narrowed to three feet at the top, giving it a tapered look. The tower featured arched, curved-stone windows at the top, and there was a walkway around the outside of the light room, also made from iron. From the ventilator ball to the bottom, the tower stood eighty-six feet tall. Housed in the tower was a Fresnel lens powered by a double-wick oil lamp. This monster piece of glass weighed 1,985 pounds and was sixty-two and a half inches tall and over three feet in diameter. The rays were refracted by the prisms of the lens and aimed in the needed direction. This lens was the invention of French

Though the Fresnel lens at Au Sable Point is no longer used, it remains so that visitors can marvel at its beauty and size. *Photo by Mikel B. Classen.*

The lighthouse upon completion in 1874. With the following announcement in the *Marquette Mining Journal*, the lighting of Au Sable Lighthouse was official: "Notice is hereby given that on or about the night of Wednesday the 19th day of August 1874, a fixed white light will be exhibited from the new brick tower at Big Sable Point." The first light keeper, Casper Kuhn, can be seen at the top of the tower. *Courtesy of the National Park Service.*

physicist Augustin-Jean Fresnel, whose combination lens-prism would revolutionize lighthouses everywhere. It meant that even the smallest flame could send out a strong and piercing beam. The light at Au Sable would be able to be seen for seventeen miles across the water.

As autumn rolled around, the partially constructed light station's purpose for being played out right in front of it. Sailing from Marquette at the time, a ship named the *Union*, one of several with that name at the time, was headed toward Au Sable when it was overtaken by a swift gale from behind. The waves and wind rose, and the *Union* was driven onto the reef. The captain, D.L. Stearns, ordered his crew to dump all the cargo they were carrying on deck. The cargo was ore, so it was heavy. They tossed everything that they could, hoping it would lift them off the rocks. For a few minutes, it seemed like it might work, but as the heavy ship began to move, the wind caught hold and tore it away and then back onto the rocks. This time, realizing there was no saving the *Union*, Captain Stearns got his crew safely to shore. Within a few days, there was little of the ship left. It had been broken to pieces by the pounding waves.

The following year saw the finishing touches applied to the station. The tower was completed, as was the residence. On July 7, a boat came to the dock and out stepped a man. The first light keeper had come to Au Sable. Casper Kuhn found everything ready for him except for whitewashing the tower and some plastering inside the residence. The long-awaited light was about to shine.

Later that month, the Lighthouse Board released the following notice to mariners: "Notice is hereby given that on or about the night of Wednesday the 19th day of August 1874, a fixed white light will be exhibited from the new brick tower at Big [Au] Sable Point." It was official. Finally, mariners would be warned of the treacherous reef. The lighthouse that they wanted so badly would finally be lit.

On August 19, as promised, Casper Kuhn climbed the iron stairs to the light tower and lit the lard oil wick for the first time. The blackness of the night would forever be changed along "Shipwreck Coast." The bright, piercing light shot out into the darkness, a beacon for the lost and a landmark in the night.

CHAPTER 3

LIGHTHOUSE LIFE

For the first year, Casper Kuhn tended the lighthouse alone. The daily chores were basic, with activities focusing on keeping the light clean and in working order. Polishing the Fresnel lens itself was a task that took several hours. The keepers were given a book of regulations to which they were to strictly adhere. This book established a code of ethics and conduct that would define the light keepers throughout the duration of the U.S. Lighthouse Service. A light keeper's mandate was to keep the light operating at all times; failure to do so was unthinkable.

Much of the routine at Au Sable was established by Kuhn. Similar to a captain's ship's log, the keeper was required to write daily entries in a keeper's log. These provide a clear record of daily life at the lighthouse: "Wind N.W. Cloudy, cleaned lens and tower glass." The daily chores were intentionally time-consuming—it was thought that if the keeper were kept busy, the isolation would be less noticeable.

Kuhn was alone except for an occasional visit from the lighthouse tender. The lighthouse tenders were a fleet of ships that made regular stops at all the lighthouses. The *Amaranth* and the *Marigold* were the two tenders assigned to make regular stops at Au Sable Point Lighthouse. The tenders were not small ships. The *Amaranth*, which is mentioned more frequently in the light keepers' logs, was 166 feet long. It would pull along the dock at the light station and unload whatever supplies were marked for Au Sable and then proceed on its way to the next station. As difficult as Au Sable is to navigate, the tenders never ran afoul of the reef and seemed to make their regular runs in and out with little difficulty.

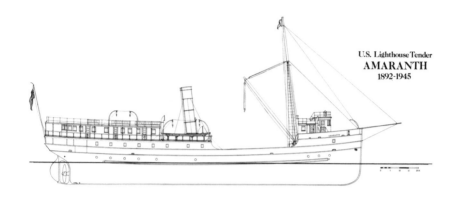

U.S. Lighthouse Tender
AMARANTH
1892-1945

The lighthouse tenders were lifelines for the keepers. Picture above is the *Amaranth*. The *Marigold*, which also put in at Au Sable on its supply route, was built with the same design. *Courtesy of U.S. Coast Guard, National Archives.*

In late September 1875, Assistant Keeper Paul Happold arrived. Happold not only helped with the constant maintenance and chores but also provided company for Kuhn. Being alone on the Lake Superior frontier was known to break men. Au Sable Point Lighthouse was constructed relatively late in comparison with other stations on Lake Superior. The first light had been constructed in 1846, and there had since been twenty-one lighthouses placed on the lake. By the time Au Sable was built, the Lighthouse Service had thirty years of experience with keepers who had been stuck in the wilderness for years on end. A light keeper had to be a strong individual both physically and mentally. There were many cases of keepers who lost their sanity. A place like Au Sable Point would not be easy to endure, and the Lighthouse Service knew this.

The following year, Kuhn and Happold built a boathouse and a storage shed. These two additions would complete the station complex, which was interconnected by wooden walkways. Au Sable is surrounded by soft sand, so the boardwalks would have been crucial for moving supplies.

It wasn't long before the isolation began to set in. The nearest town was Grand Marais, which was twelve miles by foot across the sand dunes or eight miles by boat. It made getting away from Au Sable nearly impossible. One of the early lighthouse inspectors commented after visiting Au Sable that it was "just as isolated as if it were thirty miles from land." It wore on the light keepers, and Kuhn and Happold were no exceptions. Exactly two years after they had arrived, on July 8, 1876, both men resigned from the Lighthouse Service. They had obviously had enough of Au Sable Point.

Assistant Light Keeper Ed Parker and his children posing in one of the U.S. Coast Guard boats that were used to deliver supplies. *Courtesy of the National Park Service.*

The Lighthouse Service decided to try a different approach and hired Napoleon Beedon to replace Kuhn. Beedon arranged to have his wife, Mary, appointed as assistant light keeper. Beedon was a twenty-year veteran of the Lighthouse Service and was well accustomed to lighthouse life and the isolation that accompanied it. His wife had accompanied him to some of his other light station appointments, and they seemed like a good choice. (Husband-and-wife teams—and women in general—were not unusual in the Lighthouse Service. The women in the service were just as dedicated as their male counterparts. There are many cases in which the women handled all the lighthouse duties in times of sickness or the deaths of their spouses.) The Beedons arrived in July and settled into their routine.

As autumn closed in, the couple was about to receive their initiation into life at Au Sable. Beginning on the first of October, a six-day storm ripped through the area. The log entries describe what it was like to ride it out:

> *October 1—West gale cloudy, snowing and rain and hail, cold, freezing snow, frost cold.*
> *October 2—North North West gale raining, heavy all times and cold. Some hail, cold.*

October 3—AM West gale snowing heavy, cold. PM Gale cloudy, not so cold, wind. Fresh brees [sic].

October 4—AM East gale, snowing heavy, cold. PM W.N. West gale snowing and rain, hail, cold.

October 5—AM N. West gale of snowing, thick, freezing. PM N. West gale of wind, snowing, thick, cold.

October 6—Wind west gale all times snowing thick. All times it beats all the sights I saw all there on night of the 6th. I had to put a small lamp under the burner to keep it from freezing up on the night of the 5th. The bank washed away 10 feet above the high water mark. It beats all the storms that I have ever seen on Lake Superior as Light Keeper for over 20 years in the month of October. I never saw such wether [sic] *during the last 20 year and over.*

As if in competition with itself, Lake Superior had one more tantrum to throw that year. The Beedons were about to have their world shaken. It was in early December when they experienced the force of Au Sable Point again. On December 8, 1876, Beedon wrote that there had been "AM South light brees [*sic*] cloudy, snowing and freezing." By evening, the weather had deteriorated into a vicious storm. Beedon wrote, "PM 5 o'clock, almost a hurricane, frightful storm. It blew down 50 trees or more close by the lighthouse, and I thought that the lighthouse and tower would be blown down as they shook like a leaf. The wind was NN West, snowing and freesing [*sic*]. It was the worst storm I ever saw on Lake Superior."

When it was all over, the storm had devastated the surrounding area. The trees had snapped and broken all around the station. Fortunately, it was the end of the season, and it was time to close up. The downed trees would be there in the spring, waiting to be cleared out. It would take Beedon the better portion of the following year to clean them all up. It had been a storm of epic proportions, something that occurred at Au Sable Point with some frequency.

There were some calmer moments as well, such as a rare early spring in 1878: "I never saw such beautiful wether [*sic*] as has been through the month of April. There has not been any ice on Lake Superior any time to hinder boats running and was very little snow all winter—some thing that never was known on Lake Superior before the oldest inhabitants. The earliest steamer up the lake to my knowledge before this spring was on the 18th day of April. The steamer was *North Star* from Detroit." Life at Au

Sable wasn't always hunkering down for the next blow. It did have its quiet moments—sometimes too quiet.

Recognizing the problem of isolation and solitude, the Lighthouse Service instituted a circulating library that allowed the stations to have small libraries wherein the books would be exchanged periodically. These became a part of the supply deliveries of the lighthouse tenders. In 1878, Au Sable received its library. It came in the form of square wooden boxes that could be stacked as shelves. Books and literature would always be a part of life at the light stations.

In that same year, there was a forest fire that threatened the station. Beedon submitted a request for extra pay for fighting it. In response to his request, the Lighthouse Service wrote, "It will be seen that Mr. Beedon states that he has made improvements in the nature of clearing the land around the lighthouse structures at the station where he has been employed, thus saving the public property from destruction when the surrounding forests have been on fire, for which service he thinks he is entitled to compensation." It is unclear whether he ever received anything, and this might have led to the Beedons' resignation. In a note left in the log, Beedon sounds a bit unappreciated for all of his efforts: "N. Beedon has been in the employ of the government for 18 years. I have been instrumental in saving many a person from a watery grave during the time I have been in the employ of the government. I have cleared up many an acre of land for the government. I have cleared up five different lighthouse stations that I found in a state of wilderness." One thing is clear: whether it was due to the isolation, nature's violence at Au Sable or the fact that they were simply fed up with government service, the Beedons resigned from the Lighthouse Service in August 1879. The couple had lasted only one year longer than Kuhn and Happold.

The day the Beedons resigned, there was a dense fog. Offshore, a schooner named the *Annie Coleman* was feeling its way through the fog heading for Marquette. As the schooner sailed over the reef, it struck bottom on the sandstone rock. The ship jolted and shook, but it wasn't stuck. Captain George Wilson thought they had gotten lucky and ordered the crew to continue on. But below deck in the hold, they were taking on water, and it wasn't long before the *Annie Coleman* started going down. The crew abandoned ship and made it safely to shore, where they then decided to walk the seventy miles to Marquette. Three days later, they made it and reported the loss of the ship.

Once again, the Lighthouse Service was faced with the problem of trying to replace the light keepers at Au Sable. And again it went for something different—a father-and-son team. In 1879, Frederick W. Boesler and

Frederick Jr. became the next tenders of the light at Au Sable. The pair settled into their routine well, and all seemed to be going smoothly. "The Government visited the Big Sable Light House Station and found everything correct," they recorded in the log on September 20. Later in the year, the rest of the family arrived. On September 28, 1879, Boesler Sr. noted in the log, "My family arrived here on the 28th of September 1879 and I feel contented with my lonely station."

The following year saw more maintenance on the tower and building. The original roof was made of cedar shingles, which would have needed constant replacing in the high winds at Au Sable. Boesler wrote, "Mr. J. Lauzan arrived here at Big Sable L.H. the 3rd of July with three employees for painting the tower and other improvements and left on the 15th day of July 1880."

Ships came and went from the light station. Maintenance of the docks was very important. The light keepers and crews would rebuild them, and Lake Superior would try to knock them back down. The supply ships and lighthouse tenders were the only connection the lighthouse had with the outside world. Boesler mentions clearly the importance of their comings and goings: "The supply vessel arrived here at the light house on the 18th day of

An early photo of Au Sable Point Lighthouse taken before the additions. The lighthouse keeper and his family are standing in front. It is evident that clearing the trees was still an ongoing process. *Courtesy of Superior View Studio.*

July 1880 [with] the supplies for the Light House Department. The steamer *Dahlia* visited Big Sable Light Station on the 27th of July 1882 and furnished us with supplies and new kerosene lamps." These visits were important not only because they resupplied the lighthouse but also because they provided company. Even if it were just for a few hours, the arrivals broke up the days and alleviated the feeling of loneliness.

Boesler Sr. was something of a horticulturalist. He records in the log in 1881 that "I the keeper grafted 24 fruit trees, 12 of cherry and 12 of apples, the first part of May 1881." Fresh fruit growing on site would have been a monumental improvement for future residents at the point.

Au Sable Point had been relatively peaceful over the years since the light had first been lit. But in other sections of the "Shipwreck Coast," some of the "accidents" had taken on frightening proportions. All around Au Sable, and particularly to the east toward Whitefish Point, ships and men were lost with alarming regularity. More needed to be done.

The sinking of the *Annie Coleman* had been the first real incident at Au Sable in several years. But that was about to change. With drastic increases in shipping ore from Marquette and lumber products from Munising, it was only a matter of time before Au Sable Point would lay claim to some of those ships.

In early 1882, the steamer *General Franz Sigel* or *General Sigel*—there is some dispute over the name—was on its way to Sault Ste. Marie. What isn't disputed is that it ran aground at Au Sable during another violent gale. One man was lost, having drowned in the churning lake. The rest of the crew made it to shore. One source says that the ship broke up on the reef and was listed as lost. Another source says it was pulled free with $1,000 worth of damage.

Frequently, the light keepers would walk the shoreline. On occasion, they would find things that had washed up—the remains of an accident and, every once in awhile, some useful things. An entry in the log gives an example: "Found an Indian bark canoe on the beach Aug. 15th, 1882 with a box of supplies in it."

In October of that same year, Au Sable got the best of Boesler's son. He left, and the position of assistant keeper was "abolished" from the lighthouse ledger. No reason is given for the son's departure, but Boesler Sr. continued on alone.

Au Sable Point itself was a battle for the light keepers even when doing the most basic things. This fact is illustrated by one of the entries in the station log: "Foggy, light changeable wind. I was boating wood today and swamped the scow with a load of wood and lost half of my wood." Moments like these could be trying for men alone in the wilderness. Previous entries show Boesler had been sawing that wood for several days. Alone.

Later in the following month, one of Lake Superior's notorious November gales struck. A two-masted schooner named *Eclipse* was caught in the violence. The temperature was below freezing, and snow and sleet were pummeling the ship. The icy water of Superior crashed over the sides and the bow, soaking the men. Suddenly the ship ran onto Au Sable reef, which tore the hull wide open. The *Eclipse* began sinking fast. The men scrambled up the riggings to save themselves. One man drowned as the men began to try for shore. The rest made it to shore safely. The *Eclipse* seemed to have been destined for Au Sable Point. It had become stranded there in 1880 and 1881 but was pulled free to continue on its way. Three years in a row it had run afoul of the point, but this time was the last. Now it would remain there permanently. With more loss of life, the *Eclipse* illustrated the deadly dangers that were still present at Au Sable Point itself. The lighthouse seemed to help, but much was still lacking in regards to maritime safety.

Shipping season on the lakes was short. Lake Superior would begin to freeze in October and November. By December, the bays and harbors were frozen enough that sailing in and out of them was impossible. Shipping would grind to a standstill. It wouldn't be until May or June that the ice would clear out enough for shipping to resume. Depending on the year, five or six months could be lost annually due to winter ice. The worst storms would hit in the spring and fall, but they could hit anytime. Avoiding the dangerous weather was not possible.

On July 4, 1883, Au Sable Point was again shrouded in fog. In the distance, a wooden freighter named *Mary Jarecki* was lost in the mists. Captain Anthony Everett searched for a way through the fog but had completely lost track of where he was. In an attempt to get past the dense fog, the *Mary Jarecki* sailed at full steam. Somehow the ship got turned toward the shore and, with a full head of steam, ran onto the bank, its propellers churning the water hard. The bow of the ship hit the beach with a scrape and crunch that shot through the entire vessel. The front of the ship squealed to a halt, resting a full three feet out of the water. The *Mary Jarecki* had beached and beached badly. If it had gone another mile, it would have torn its hull apart on the reef.

Boesler, who could see the *Mary Jarecki* well from the light tower at Au Sable, made a note of the incident in the log: "On the 4th day of July

The *Mary Jarecki* getting ready to take on a tow of schooners. *Courtesy of the National Park Service.*

1883 the steam barge *Mary Jarecki* run on the shore. She is a total wreck here. Commander was Captain Everett from Kenosha, Wisconsin. No lives were lost."

Captain Everett, not willing to give up on his ship, traveled to Sault Ste. Marie to initiate salvage operations. He hired the tug *Mystic*, returned to Au Sable Point with pumps and crew and retrieved what he could. They pumped for a full day and night but had no luck. The *Mary Jarecki* had too big a hole in its hull, and it was surmised that the hull's frame might have been fractured as well. The owners gave up the ship, but that wasn't the end of the salvage attempts.

The *Mary Jarecki* was now a target for salvage. If it could be refloated, the ship would belong to the salvager. A tug named the *Otsego* came with pumps, a diver and a lighter barge named *Vampire* to work on the wreck. The diver went down and patched the hull as well as possible, and then they set the pumps to working. For three days and two nights, they ran the pumps. The water inside the ship never fell an inch, and they subsequently gave up.

One month later, another attempt was made with all the optimism that could be mustered. The *Marquette Mining Journal* reported, "The wrecking tug *Kate Williams* has been at work on the wrecked propeller *Mary Jarecki* for the past couple of weeks and she may have got off by this time. The tug was provided with a full wrecking outfit and a force of divers. The bottom was found to be in a badly damaged state, being pounded full of bad holes, which the divers were patching up at the last report we had from there. When this was done, six large steam pumps were to be set [to] work pumping the water out of her and an attempt then made to raise her with pontoons. The captain in charge anticipated no difficulty in raising her and thinks that he will deliver her at the dry docks in a short time."

But the *Mary Jarecki* never moved, and the salvage operation was given up. The ship was offered up for sale. No one bought it.

On September 25, Frederick Boesler Sr. watched the *Mary Jarecki* from the light tower. The wind was blowing hard, and Lake Superior was beating the stranded ship mercilessly. Boesler stood and watched as the ship was pounded to pieces. The shoreline was its end, and it lies there still today for all to see. Boesler's simple entry was the *Mary Jarecki*'s epitaph: "*Mary Jarecki* went to pieces from the 24th to the 25th of September 1883."

Boesler resigned the following year. He, too, had had enough of Au Sable Point. It was time to move on. This brought to the lighthouse Gus Gigandet and his wife, Mary. They were accompanied by George Zenker, the assistant keeper. On May 21, their first day, Gus wrote in the log, "I and my wife arrived here and the assistant on the 21st day of May 1884, and I feel contented and satisfied with the station." The couple and their assistant fell into their duties and routines easily.

The Gigandets seemed to adjust well to life at the point—the isolation that had taken its toll on their predecessors didn't seem to bother them. Gus enjoyed trout fishing and bragged that he'd caught 144 brook trout. The abundance of game in the area could also add to the food supplies. Between the now-developing fruit trees and wild game in the area, the light station was becoming self-sustaining.

But there were moments of mishaps along the way: "On the 16th day of May 1885 we accidentally lost the anker [*sic*] of the sail boat belonging to the station. It was lost near the shore and we expect to find it. It was blowing fresh breese [*sic*] from the south." Another incident was reported on September 1: "On September 1st, the Assistant Keeper Mr. George Wilson accidentally lost the sail, mast, rudder, and foot board of the sail boat, coming from Grand Marais. It was blowing a moderate breese [*sic*] from the S.E."

Wreckage of the *Mary Jarecki* along the shore at Au Sable Point. Pieces of this ship are strewn for hundreds of feet along Lake Superior. *Courtesy of the National Park Service.*

Mostly, the days were routine and involved more upkeep. Gigandet wrote about the work: "Some painting done at the out side of the Big Sable Light House. The top of the tower and the first deck and sealing the second deck, for the house all the window shutters, frame and sash and outside windows. We put in 80 hours work in painting the above mentioned places."

Though no wrecks occurred at Au Sable, storms continued to rage across Lake Superior. In November 1886, Gigandet wrote, "One of the heaviest gales from the northwest with a blinding snowstorm I have ever experienced." In July of the following year, he wrote, "The wind blew so strong that it caused the tower to shake hard."

Au Sable Point Lighthouse's intended function was to be a beacon for ships, but matters of life and death can come from any direction. In 1887, Gus Gigandet wrote of an incident that came from the depths of the woods: "On August the 8th, an old gentleman, a watch man in a lumber camp 4 miles west of the station, came here to the lighthouse at 2 o'clock PM, sick and unable to go farther. It was blowing a gale wind from the south so we could not take him away in a boat, and at 9:30 PM he was dead. The man was about 70 years of age and belonging to Canada. I notified the Justis [sic] of Grand Marais the next day who came and took the corpse away to Grand Marais to be buried." Au Sable Point Lighthouse was a shelter for all who needed it.

At this point, ship traffic was again increasing exponentially. In 1890, it was estimated that nearly 2 million tons of ore had passed by Au Sable Point. Iron ore and copper had turned places like Duluth, Calumet and Marquette into boomtowns. More and more mines were being dug, and the Keweenaw Peninsula had copper mines that were flourishing. The iron ranges of Duluth and Marquette were also growing, with old mines expanding and new mines being dug annually. Fortunes were being made, and immigrant workers from places like Finland, Sweden, Italy and Cornwall were flocking to the region seeking work and fortunes. There had even been strikes of gold north of Marquette, which fueled the stories of the wealth of the Lake Superior frontier. Like in other parts of the country, particularly the West, a migration was occurring.

It wasn't simply minerals and lumber that were sailing past Au Sable and along the dangerous coastline; it was an entire population bound for new land and opportunities—men and families who would explode the seams of these young boomtowns. They were important as the labor and citizens of the future. These people would mean the success of the mining barons who were the backbones of these growing cities. Calumet, in the Keweenaw Peninsula, was well on its way to becoming the largest city in Michigan.

More had to be done to ensure the safety of the ships. Since ship traffic was forced to hug the treacherous southern shore when the gales from the north would strike, foghorns became a topic of discussion. And with the fogs that Au Sable was notorious for, it was a part of that conversation. The Lighthouse Board wanted fog signals on Lake Superior.

The lighthouse had been in operation for more than ten years. The current lighthouse inspector, Commander Horace Elmer, felt that the entire station was showing signs of age and use, so he dispatched a work crew to the station to "spruce things up." Keeping up with the weathering that took place along the Lake Superior shore while also effectively manning the light tower was difficult for a couple light keepers.

In the late 1800s, some of the ships became passenger vessels. Newspapers like the *Mining Journal* frequently published firsthand accounts of ship travel and the wondrous natural sights of Lake Superior. Passenger ships became more and more popular, and their appearance was frequent. Passenger lines touting destinations in the Great Lakes were quite lucrative. With Mackinac Island added as the second U.S national park in 1875, travel into the region boomed.

Stories of the Pictured Rocks and their overwhelming beauty, as well as the breathtaking nature of Lake Superior as a whole, created early tourism. Regularly scheduled passenger ships from Detroit, Chicago and Port Huron would sail to Mackinac Island and "Points North," as the advertising proclaimed, "hitting all of the highlights for your sight-seeing pleasure." The Soo Locks, which are still considered a marvel of engineering and a tourist attraction, were promoted along with the Grand Sable Dunes and the Pictured Rocks as trip highlights. These ships would carry quite a diversity of passengers. Poor immigrants searching for jobs and the "better life" would often find themselves sitting next to rich travelers leisurely touring the world. The vast wilderness was filling up quickly.

It was on an evening in July 1891 that just such a ship was sailing offshore of Grand Sable Dunes heading for Au Sable. The cold water of Lake Superior was reacting with the heat of summer and the hot air of the dunes, creating a dense fog. Captain Green was sounding the whistle of his ship, *Empire State*, in an attempt to hear where the shore was located by listening to the echo. Suddenly, the echo wasn't right. The captain adjusted his course to the north, thinking that he was close to Au Sable Point. He was correct. Almost immediately, he hit the reef nearly a mile offshore.

The lake was fairly calm. Captain Green decided to try to back the *Empire State* off the rocky shoal. He kept at it into the night until the wind started to kick up. Green, realizing his efforts were futile, turned his attention to his passengers and crew. He gave the order for everyone to head for shore. The lifeboats were launched, and all the passengers and crew made it to the beach safely.

At 3:00 a.m., there was a banging on the lighthouse door. Gus Gigandet opened the door and stared out at sixty-four wet and cold people. They were all chattering at each other, creating a noisy spectacle in the darkness. Twenty-four passengers and forty crewmen had all been drenched when they climbed out of the lifeboats. They were in need of shelter.

The residence at Au Sable wasn't built to accommodate sixty-four extra people, but the Gigandets didn't let that deter them. They housed and fed them all. The twenty-four passengers stayed at the lighthouse until the following night, when a ship named the *India* picked them up. The *Empire State*'s crew of forty stayed for two more days. The Gigandets provided their best hospitality in what had to be a difficult situation.

The Au Sable log records the unexpected visit: "On the 17th of July, the passenger propeller *Empire State* run on the reef 1 mile N.W. of the Light House, bound east, in thick fog. She had on board 24 passengers, 16 male and 8 female, and 40 in the crew, and all came ashore to the light house on the 18th at 3:30 A.M. It was blowing a fresh breeze from the North West. All passengers got passage a board passenger propeller *India* at 8 o'clock P.M. on the 18th. The crew did not leave the lighthouse till the 20th at 4 o'clock A.M."

Though many thought the *Empire State* was stuck for good on the reef, Captain Martin Swain and his tug *Favorite* had other ideas. Swain brought along a diver, who systematically patched all the holes and leaks in the ship. The *Empire State* was carrying seven hundred tons of copper ore from the Keweenaw, a cargo of considerable worth. Often the passenger ships carried cargo along with their fares, maximizing the ship's profits for each voyage. Using a lighter barge, the captain and his crew were able to remove about half the copper. They then began to pump the ship dry. The reef had a firm grip on the ship, which had settled on the bottom. Eventually, they lightened the ship enough to refloat it, freeing it from the reef. On July 22, just ten days after the grounding, the *Empire State* was on its way back toward the Soo, steaming under its own power. Again, the lighthouse log recorded the incident: "On the 22nd of July, the *Empire State* was pulled off the reef at 10:30 P.M. bound for Sault Ste. Marie."

The following year, the Lighthouse Board requested an appropriation of $5,500 to place a fog signal at Au Sable. The light had been an improvement, but in the frequent fogs, it wasn't much of a help. The Lighthouse Board pled its case: "This important light station is on the southern shore of Lake Superior, about halfway between Marquette and Whitefish Point. The entire traffic of Marquette, which, it was stated, was some 1,772,400 tons in 1890, passes close to this station, and in time of southerly gales the whole commerce of Lake Superior hugs the south shore. A steam fog signal is required to complete the satisfactory equipment of the station. It is estimated that it can be established at a cost not exceeding $5,500, and it is recommended that an appropriation of this amount be made therefor." Congress agreed that the need was there and passed an act approving the establishment of the fog signal on February 15, 1893. But there was one problem: Congress neglected to appropriate the money. The foghorn would not be forthcoming. Au Sable was instead sent a hand-crank signal, which required a man to crank it continuously until the fog had lifted and it became clear again.

In 1892, there was a change at Au Sable: Mary Gigandet officially became the assistant light keeper. Since the Gigandets had arrived, there had been four assistant keepers assigned to the job. They didn't last long at Au Sable Point, though one of the assistants, William Laviate, would stay near Au Sable in the winter and work in one of the lumber camps that had sprung up in the woods surrounding the light station.

It is likely that in the case of the single keeper living in the same quarters as the married couple, the situation might have only enhanced the loneliness. Whatever the reason, Mary and Gus were alone at Au Sable. The pair had now lived there longer than anyone else. They seemed to have made it their home, and they treated those who arrived there, by whatever means, with all the hospitality and grace of their own residence.

July can spawn some fast and violent thunderstorms. On July 24, 1893, there was a vicious lightning storm. Torrential rain and rolling thunder assailed the light station. As the storm reached its peak, lightning struck the light tower. Gigandet wrote in the log, "During a thunder storm July 24th the lightning struck the tower at 9 o'clock P.M., boring two holes in the bottom of the tower, right at the foot of the stairs, and burning and damaging the paint in several places about the floor." Even the great tower couldn't remain unscathed from the fury of Superior.

Later that year, another storm hit that also caused damage to the station. It had been a year of powerful storms that impressed even the keeper who had seen so many. Gus Gigandet wrote, "On the 14th day of October 1893 the top of the boat landing crib got washed away during a hurricane gale from the north, the biggest storm I have seen for twenty two years."

In previous years, the lamp at Au Sable had burned lard and sperm (whale) oil. Because of the oil's stability, it was stored in the residence cellar. During this time, the Lighthouse Service began converting all the lighthouses to kerosene, which unfortunately was stored in the same way. That error was learned the hard way after several fires broke out at light stations. At that point, it was wisely decided that storage sheds located away from the main buildings would be a better idea.

In the 1880s, a systematic plan was created to upgrade every station with an oil storage building. It was 1895 before they made it to Au Sable. That summer, a crew put up a fireproof brick oil storage building with a metal roof fifty feet behind the station. Though it got volatile fuel out of the house, the change of having to bring it in opposed to going down to the basement, particularly in bad weather or deep snow, couldn't have been seen as an improvement at Au Sable.

CHAPTER FOUR

CHANGES

pproximately twelve miles away in Grand Marais, things were changing
quickly. The Alger Smith Company had moved in and was buying the
local lumbering concern. The company had been logging the woods
from Manistique to Seney, twenty-five miles south, but now set its eyes on
Grand Marais to the north and its natural harbor.

The Alger Smith Company was founded in Detroit by Russell A. Alger
and M.S. Smith. Having logged the lumber out of the Saginaw and Bay City
areas, the company had been working its way north using the Titabawassee
River to run its logs down into Lake Huron. Alger Smith was known for
going into an area and cleaning it out of all usable lumber, particularly the
mammoth white pines that filled the state. In a very short amount of time,
the company would purchase huge tracts of land, log them and then move
on. In most cases, this process took less than a decade.

Having logged most of the available land in the Lower Peninsula,
the company naturally set its sights on the Upper Peninsula. It began
purchasing large holdings in the eastern Upper Peninsula south of Lake
Superior. North of Manistique, from Newberry to Shingleton, became a
part of its lumbering operations. The area became known as Seney and
was fed by the Fox River, whose waters eventually reached Lake Michigan.
Because of a natural oddity, the longest rivers in the Upper Peninsula flow
south to Lake Michigan, not Lake Superior. On the southern shore of
Lake Superior, the sources of all the rivers that flow into it are within no
more than twenty miles of the shore.

Consequently, in the southern and central portions of the Upper Peninsula, logs could be floated for miles down the streams and their tributaries. When it came to the prime lumber of the Lake Superior region, however, the streams could be used only for the immediate area. In this region, Lake Superior itself would have to be utilized, and in many cases, inventive ideas had to be employed to overcome the extremes of its rugged shore.

The kidney-shaped harbor of Grand Marais, the only safe harbor for fifty miles, was a natural choice. There had been a sawmill there for years, but the business had dried up and was now sitting fallow. Alger Smith saw this as an ideal opportunity and not only purchased the sawmill but also built a railroad leading from Seney to Grand Marais in 1894. Before the railroad, the only way into Grand Marais was by ship. The railroad changed everything. Grand Marais exploded with workers and passengers coming to the lumber town by both rail and ship. Alger Smith's own men migrated north, filling the woods and hiring any other able-bodied men they came across.

Alger Smith purchased most of the forestlands surrounding Grand Marais to the east and west, including much of the land that surrounded Au Sable Point, while other smaller new companies grabbed the parcels that were left. By 1896, Grand Marais's population had risen from 177 to 2,000. The shoreline became packed with lumber, stacked anywhere there was available space. Next to logs and sawed boards were mountains of shingles. Every inch of shoreline was a staging area for the lumber. At any one time, there could be as many as thirty ships crowding the little harbor.

Suddenly, all along the harbor and bay, lumber operations were springing up in all of their facets. The sawmills were running day and night cutting up the millions of board feet being brought in by Alger Smith's loggers. The Devil's Log Slide was constructed down the side of Grand Sable Dunes. This monster of a log chute began at the top of Grand Sable Dunes, more than three hundred feet above Lake Superior. Logs would shoot down from the top at a breakneck speed into the small bay created where Au Sable Point meets the sand dunes. The incline of the slide was steep, more than thirty-five degrees, and was known to burst into flames from the friction of the logs, hence the slide's name. One didn't want to be anywhere near those logs when they came down the chute. There is one story of a log that hit and skipped on the water, striking a man standing in a boat. One second he was there, and the next it was only his shoes!

Logs from the white pine forests that abounded in the surrounding countryside were piled at the tops of the sand dunes. They were then sent

The view from the Log Slide Overlook of the immense Grand Sable Dunes stretching to the horizon. In the distance at the very tip is Grand Marais. The overlook once was a giant log chute that sent logs screaming down into Lake Superior. The logs went down so fast that they sometimes caught on fire, earning the chute its nickname of Devil's Log Slide. *Photo by Mikel B. Classen.*

down the slide to Superior and gathered into large groups. Each group would then be encircled by a boom and towed into Grand Marais to the sawmills. These booms would hold hundreds of logs that the tugs would then have to pull across Lake Superior into the harbors.

At the mouth of the Hurricane River, on the other side of the light station, logs were stacked in mammoth piles. Ships would come in daily and take the piles to Grand Marais, carefully maneuvering around the reef. The logs were piled near the wreck of the *Mary Jarecki*, and the ships would have had to maneuver around what was left of the ship, a constant reminder of the fate that could be theirs.

John Gillece ran the Alger Smith lumber camps at the log slide and the Hurricane River. Known as "Daylight Johnny," he ran a crew of about one hundred men and had a reputation for getting them to cut trees faster than

Piles of logs were stacked at the mouth of the Hurricane River for pickup to be rafted to Grand Marais. The man in the boat is looking at the wreck of the *Mary Jarecki*, which can be seen in the foreground. *Courtesy of Mikel B. Classen.*

anyone else. Gillece was well liked by his men, and they worked hard for him, cutting down every white pine possible. Since they worked in winter, daylight hours were short. That meant being in the woods at the crack of dawn and quitting as close to dark as possible.

Gillece got his nickname, "Daylight Johnny," because he once changed working hours during an emergency spring breakup. The snow was melting fast, and the horses would no longer be able to skid logs without the snow. At stake was 1 million board feet of lumber. If the lumber didn't make it to the Manistique Railway, it would rot where it lay and the men wouldn't get paid for their winter work. Essentially authorizing overtime and having his workers go from before dawn until after dusk, they were able to get every last log out of the woods and to the railway. He paid his men a bonus when it was all done.

Sullivan's Landing was a little past the Hurricane River. Named after Thomas G. Sullivan, it, too, became a staging area for logs. At Sullivan's logging camp alone, there were two crews of 150 men harvesting the white pine from the area. They had three yokes of oxen and twenty teams of horses. The Kingston Plains, one of the former white pine forests, was logged over three times and to this day has never grown back. Huge white pine stumps still dot the landscape like tombstones at Arlington Cemetery.

The Sullivan camp lasted only three years, but in that time, the crews cut over 50 million board feet of white pine, all of which was sent to the shoreline and rafted to Grand Marais, Sault Ste. Marie or even the lower Great Lakes. With dozens of other operations doing the same thing all along the shore, ships weren't just sailing past Au Sable anymore. It was now becoming their destination.

It is hard to comprehend exactly how much was going on around Au Sable Point in this era. There were thousands of workers in the surrounding woods, although no one really knows the exact number. We do know that over three thousand acres of white pine was cut in the vicinity. Afterward, the loggers moved west, following the forests.

Though most of the logs were brought out in the winter, they would sit until spring, when the lake would open back up and the ships could get in to take the logs to the mill. And while Au Sable had always been quiet and lonely, its surroundings now bustled with activity. Tugs were coming in on both sides of the point and leaving with their booms of logs. On the horizon, more ships would sail by carrying the usual ore. But now, with sawmills running day and night, ships were also carrying loads of lumber and shingles.

To get more from the trips, old schooners were refitted with steam or used as barges. They would create what they called a "tow," in which one main ship would run a line to a ship or ships behind it. Sometimes there were as many as many as six or seven ships in a tow. When a storm arose, the situation became extremely dangerous and often resulted in shipwrecks.

The *Volunteer* was a two-masted schooner that had been refitted for use as a barge. Owned by the Alger Smith Company, it was loaded with supplies for the Sullivan's Landing camp. The ship was overtaken by a northwest gale between the Hurricane River and Sullivan's Landing. The captain lost control of the ship, which grounded on the shallows at the shore. Lake Superior then proceeded to pound the ship to pieces. Gigandet wrote in the log, "The schooner *Volunteer* was wrecked on the beach 4 miles west of the light house on the 15th in a gale from the N.W."

CHAPTER 5

TRAGEDIES

S ince all of the logging took place in the winter, during the spring, summer and fall, the woods were empty. And while ships moved all around, reining in the logs and loading the ones piled on the shore, Au Sable remained apart from it all.

Gus and Mary Gigandet went on with their daily routines and kept the light shining. In 1896, they were in their twelfth year at the lighthouse. It had truly become their home. They had adjusted well and seemed to enjoy life at the point, as well as the bounty offered by its surroundings. Gus would occasionally fish and hunt while Mary tended the light and worked around the grounds.

In June of that year, the funding for the fog signal finally came through. The boilers and machinery were sent to the Detroit lighthouse depot. They didn't reach Au Sable until September, however, so a work party was postponed until the following year. But the foghorn itself had reached Au Sable, and it had to be covered until the following spring.

The weather in the late fall can be a dangerous thing, and in October 1896, Gus Gigandet became ill. His wife, Mary, kept the light going and tried to care for him at the same time. It was an insurmountable task. The chill of autumn had struck deep, and Gus was getting worse. Mary diligently continued keeping the light, and after two weeks, Gus Gigandet died. A brief statement of his death can be found in the log: "On the 29th day of Oct. Gus Gigandet, the principal Keeper, died after an illness of two weeks."

Mary Gigandet continued on. She was the keeper now, and she finished out the season. The Gigandets' life at Au Sable had been pleasant. The isolation had never been a problem for them. Instead, they had enjoyed the lighthouse life, but they had enjoyed it as a couple. When the season was over, Mary resigned.

In 1897, Mary was replaced by Herbert Weeks and his assistant keeper, James Dooley. Most of the lighthouses being upgraded to the new steam fog signals now had two assistant keepers to deal with the increased workload of feeding the boilers, but Au Sable seems to have been an exception. It appears that Weeks and Dooley were expected to do the work of three men.

Immediately that spring, work began on the installation of the long-awaited fog signal. Gone would be the days of the endless hours of cranking. The steam signal was big, however, and it was going to take major construction to get it up and operating. A new crib and seawall were needed, and a building would have to be raised to house the signal horn and pipes necessary to carry lake water to produce the steam that blew the horn. The materials and work party arrived on the lighthouse tender *Amaranth*. Herbert Weeks recorded the activity in the log: "The *Amaranth* stopped hear [*sic*] on her way up and unloaded a fog signal for this station. The assistant left the station at 4:15 to go to Grand Marais for groceries. We have twelve men working here putting in the fog signal." A few days later, Weeks recorded, "The *Amaranth* arrived at this station at 8:40 with brick and lumber for the fog signal." The job ran into the following day: "The *Amaranth* finished unloading her cargo of brick and lumber for the fog signal today at six o'clock and started for the Sault."

When the signal building was completed, it was equipped with twin ten-inch locomotive steam whistles fired by horizontal boilers. These whistles would become important to the future of the lighthouse. A water pipe was placed in a timber crib and sunk offshore to supply the boilers, which were fed by a force pump. A seawall was also erected to prevent erosion to the shore around the new signal building. The dock was repaired, extended and raised, and the wooden sidewalks were replaced by concrete. The new fog signal was set in place and tested. The fog signal was an amazing thing—it was large and powerful, able to be heard for twenty-five miles across the water. When the horn would blast, the surface of Lake Superior would ripple. The peal of the foghorn was deafening.

The year 1897 was a long one for Light Keeper Herbert Weeks. With all the construction and improvements, he had been able to keep busy: "We whitewashed the seller and the oil house yesterday. The men finished the floor in the fog signal." A few days later, he wrote, "Seen one large whaleback steamer going down the lake. The first one we have seen. We was [*sic*] cutting wood for the fog signal." There was even an unexpected occasional visitor: "We had two men here for dinner today. They had been lost in the woods for 12 hours."

With the end of the year setting in, shipping ran longer into the winter than usual. Weeks was away from home and his family. Though the family had spent the summer months there, they had left at the beginning of October. When December rolled around, shipping continued. It appeared that Weeks would spend the winter at the lighthouse. Once the snow and ice set in, there was no getting out of there, short of a twelve-mile trek on snowshoes to Grand Marais. Weeks missed his family. In the lighthouse log on December 26, 1897, he wrote, "This has been a very lonesome Christmas." Isolation and loneliness were the hard realities of Au Sable. The following year, Weeks tried to avert that loneliness and again brought his family with him.

News of war came to Au Sable in 1898. The light keepers rarely commented on happenings in the world around them, likely because their only contacts were occasional visits from the light tenders and wanderers coming in from the woods. It is likely that very little news reached the keepers during their stay at the station. One of the rare moments when it did was

A late winter scene at Au Sable Point. The brutality of winter here must have been hard to bear. Exposed to the fiercest of Lake Superior winds, Au Sable Point is in the teeth of it. *Courtesy of Superior View Studio.*

documented by Weeks, who was told of the Spanish-American conflict in Cuba on June 30, 1898. The log entry for this date expresses a common reaction for the time: "There has been some great changes during the year. Some very sad happenings. The most terrible thing was the wreck of the *Maine* and loss of the crew. But revenge is sweet and the same, and the United States will repay." Weeks reflected the sentiment that was shared by most Americans at the time over the sinking of the *Maine* in Cuba's Havana Harbor.

Before the year was out, tragedy struck Light Keeper Weeks and his family. Unfortunately, all that is known comes from one entry in the lighthouse log on September 30, 1898: "The Principal Keeper left his station to go to Grand Island at 8 am to bury one of his children. Partly clear, fresh breeze, north west." No more information is given. Weeks continued on as light keeper, putting the loss behind him.

Though the light keepers were required to keep their light burning, that was sometimes easier said than done. Often there was mechanical failure, and the keepers were expected to fix the problem and get the light back up and running. The following log entry by Weeks is telling: "I had considerable trouble with the light last night. I had to take her apart twice. There seamed [*sic*] to be some thing wrong…I could not get the float to work and I worked about 1 hour before I got it to work."

The following year saw another improvement to the complex. A tramway was constructed so that supplies from the lighthouse tenders could be moved from the dock to the signal house.

In 1900, the U.S. Life-Saving Service built a station at Grand Marais. The Life-Saving Service had been active in Lake Superior since 1875 with stations at Vermillion Point, Crisp Point, Two-Hearted River and Deer Park. All of these were situated to the east between Grand Marais and Whitefish Point. Though they couldn't prevent shipwrecks, they were able to reduce the loss of lives and were instrumental in saving many of the ships that had foundered and were recoverable or salvageable. The lifesavers worked tirelessly and lent aid in any situation they could. Now that a long-needed station had been built at Grand Marais, saving the crews from shipwrecks at Au Sable Point would be part of their duties. The light keeper at Au Sable would now be able to send out an alarm for help, as a ship-in-trouble signal was created by a series of blasts on the locomotive steam whistles installed in the signal building.

These lifesavers were amazing and intrepid men. When a ship was in distress, they would launch their "surfboats" into the highest waves, breaking through to row the crew of the foundering vessel back to shore. It was dangerous work, and the lifesavers could be lost just as easily as those they were saving.

Captain Trudell, the commander at the Grand Marais Life-Saving Station, drilled his men incessantly. For them, preparedness meant life or death, and not just their own. They could be seen daily launching their boats into the wildest surf. They pulled the oars against the force of the water and dipped into the deep trough of waves only to have to pull through the next. Captain Trudell's men were some of the finest in the service. They rescued countless men in their tenure and remain in the highest regard to this day. The lifesavers had a saying: "Regulations say we have to go out, but they don't say anything about coming back." With that, the Grand Marais "Storm Warriors" began their tenure.

For Au Sable Point, the coming of Trudell and his crew meant the light keepers were now active participants in the rescues of ships and their crews. They were now required not only to keep the light and the fog signals going but also to watch the horizon for signs of distress. The light keepers would now walk the shoreline regularly looking for signs of distress and the odd body or two that would occasionally wash ashore.

On April 9, 1902, a large steel steamer, the *Crescent City*, was towing a whaleback barge. A unique design, the "whaleback" barge was a completely enclosed cylindrical ship with a wheelhouse bridge on top. (While it looked a lot like a submarine, it was a bad thing if it submerged.) The ship and its charge were heading toward Sault Ste. Marie from Marquette laden with early season ore. In the fog, which forms easily in April with the spring sun against the icy lake, both ships became engulfed and Au Sable Point became obscured. The light keeper had gone out to fire up the foghorn at 6:00 a.m., but it took some time for the steam to build up and start blasting. At 6:15 a.m., both ships hit Au Sable reef. The foghorn had yet to blow.

Keeper Weeks sent a message to Grand Marais requesting tugs and men to help the stranded ship. In the meantime, the fog had lifted some, and the *Crescent City* was spotted by the lookout at Grand Marais. Trudell dispatched his men, who rowed to the wreck site in case their help was needed. The loads needed to be lightened to get the ships off the rocks. Trudell and his men worked alongside the crew shoveling ore over the sides of the ships. More men arrived from Grand Marais. Nearly one hundred men worked for two full days, emptying both ships one shovelful at a time.

A tug came out from Grand Marais and attempted to pull the two ships loose, but it failed. The shoveling continued until finally a second tug joined in, and both the *Crescent City* and the whaleback came free. The whaleback was badly leaking, and a gale was beginning to brew. With the weather worsening, the *Crescent City* towed the whaleback to Grand Island for temporary repairs instead of trying for the Soo. Because of the possibility of the ships foundering, the lifesaving crew followed them in their surfboat, which was tied to the stern of the whaleback. It was a forty-mile sail, and due to rough seas, the trip took seven hours. It was a wet and miserable voyage for the lifesavers, who were now stranded at Grand Island and would have to wait until the storm wore itself out before they could return to their station at Grand Marais. Fortunately, they were able to hitch a ride from one of the tugs that had helped get the barge and the *Crescent City* to Grand Island. At least the lifesavers didn't have to row back.

When the whaleback barge was examined, a diver found that the outer hull had been smashed but that the inner hull had remained intact. This is what saved the whaleback. If it had hit Au Sable just a bit harder and pierced that inner steel, it would be lying with the other wrecks claimed by the point.

Exactly one month later, on May 9, the *Lizzie A. Law* was being towed by a steamer named the *Monohansett*. Both ships were full of coal and on their way to Duluth. The *Lizzie A. Law* was a four-masted schooner. It had been a magnificent and fast ship in its prime but had since been relegated to the duties of a barge. Its old wood frame had seen a lot of wear, and the decades on the water had made the hull quite leaky. Its crew, which consisted of only five men, had difficulty keeping the pumps operating with so few hands.

As is often the case during the spring, a gale blew up. The *Monohansett* was pulling hard on the *Lizzie A. Law* when the cable that connected the two broke. The crew of the *Lizzie A. Law* were not to be daunted. Sailors to the bone, they understood their ship. They shipped its sails and, like days past, ran it before the storm. Once again, its sails billowed and men climbed the riggings. Its bow cut the water, but the building surf was proving to be too much.

This drama did not go unnoticed. Weeks and his assistant were watching at Au Sable, and they saw the *Lizzie A. Law* struggling against Lake Superior as it passed the reef about three miles out.

The crew of the *Lizzie A. Law* could no longer keep water out of the hull. The constant battering was forcing the ship to take on more water than usual, and above the deck could be heard the sounds of sails being shredded by the wind. Refusing to give up, the men dropped anchor. They hoped the ship would turn and face the squall and ride it out.

When the ship dropped anchor, the light keepers at Au Sable sent out the distress signal to Trudell and the Grand Marais lifesavers. Trudell quickly arranged for a tug to tow a surfboat to the *Lizzie A. Law*. Before they got there, however, the surf became too rough and the tug turned back, taking the lifesavers with it. On the *Lizzie A. Law*, the crew worked to keep the water in the holds from getting deeper, but they were fighting a losing battle.

Undeterred by the first attempt, Captain Trudell hired a team of horses, had his crew lash their surfboat to a wagon and then sent them out along the shore to Au Sable. By land, Au Sable is twelve miles from Grand Marais, separated by the Grand Sable Sand Dunes. The dunes butt up to the lakeshore, leaving a fairly wide strip of land that can be traveled. When the surf is high, the waves pound directly against the dunes across this strip. Large avalanches of sand will slide down with the waves, making passage treacherous at best and impassable at worst. The wagon made it about seven miles before there was no more going forward. It was from this point that the lifesavers once again decided to launch for the ship in distress. They pulled hard for the *Lizzie A. Law*, but the waves were formidable, and it took more than three hours to reach the ship. It was in deep trouble, the water being more than seven feet deep in the holds. The ropes and rigging were now encased in ice, as the temperature had dropped. Trudell decided that the most prudent thing to do was to get the crew off the ship. The lifesavers put them in the surfboats and rowed to Au Sable Point Lighthouse. It was the closest shelter from the storm, and the crew were wet and dangerously close to freezing. The lifesavers then went back to the ship and watched over it through the night.

When daylight rolled around, the lifesavers came back to shore for the crew. The *Lizzie A. Law* still sailed—but for how long? The lifesavers returned the crew to their ship and went to work on fixing a failed steam pump. Before long, it was repaired and pumping again. Trudell and his men then took the captain of the *Lizzie A. Law* into Grand Marais to secure the services of a tug so that the *Lizzie A. Law* could then be repaired. While they were gone looking for a tug, the *Monohansett* returned looking for its lost barge and towed it to Grand Island. The proud old schooner, refusing to become another victim of Au Sable Point, would sail again.

On October 1, 1903, before the end of the shipping season, Keeper Weeks had had enough. The tragedy of his child's death coupled with being separated from his family had likely factored in his difficult decision. Those in the Lighthouse Service were extremely dedicated people, and it was unusual for a keeper to leave his post before the season was over. Weeks was subsequently transferred and demoted.

His emergency replacement at the lighthouse was Otto Bufe, who arrived to finish out the season. The following year, Bufe would return with his entire family. First Assistant Orrin Young also had his family staying at the lighthouse. The year 1904 would see the long-awaited appointing of a second assistant at the lighthouse. Garfield Sweet was assigned to fill those duties, and he arrived with his family as well. Now there would be three families living in the one residence building at the light station. Strangely, the once-isolated Au Sable Point was now crowded. There were children playing while the keepers went about their routines. Family life was a full-time part of the light station.

That summer, the fog signal building had its iron smokestack replaced. Workers put in its place a forty-foot-tall brick chimney. Unfortunately, this wasn't the improvement Au Sable really needed. It needed another house. The keeper's residence had been cramped with two families in it, but now with three, the spacious three-story building that had been designed for comfort was no longer spacious or comfortable. But as the situation dictated, the families made the best of what they had. As the year wore on, it became apparent that Otto Bufe's wife was pregnant. Somehow, Bufe and his wife were able to find some privacy.

On October 4, a ship named the *Sitka* was steaming toward Au Sable Point. It was a misty day with no wind, not the usual gale that plagued the point. Overall, Lake Superior was quiet. No one is sure why, but on that day, the *Sitka* ran hard onto Au Sable reef.

Fortunately, the incident was seen by another passing ship, the *Hunter*. As the *Hunter* sailed into Grand Marais, its crew signaled the lifesaving station that the *Sitka* needed help. Captain Trudell roused his men, and soon they were in their surfboat rowing for Au Sable Point. It took them three hours to row nine miles.

When they arrived, it was obvious that the *Sitka* was in real trouble. The ship was taking on water in a number of places, and the assessment wasn't good. Trudell advised the crew to give up and abandon ship, but the captain, F.E. Johnson, didn't want to. He insisted that Trudell take several messages requesting tugs back to Grand Marais to be taken to Sault Ste. Marie. He was certain that if he had help, the *Sitka* could get free.

Trudell had a different plan. Instead of rowing the surfboat back to Grand Marais, he had his men row to the Au Sable Point Lighthouse. He sent one of his men with the messages back to Grand Marais on foot. He then had the rest of his men camp on the beach next to the lighthouse, where they could watch the *Sitka* through the night. By the early morning, the waves started to kick up, and Lake Superior was getting rough.

Trudell, thinking that by now the *Sitka*'s crew might be ready to come ashore, had his men head out to the ship. He was right. They'd had enough and were ready to come off the ship. They launched the *Sitka*'s two lifeboats and, with the aid of the surfboat, were able to get all seventeen crewmen off, as well as their baggage. They were deposited on the beach in front of the lighthouse.

The crew of the *Sitka* walked overland to Grand Marais, leaving all their luggage at the lighthouse. It was certainly the better choice for those living in the light station, as accommodating seventeen extra people would have been difficult. It was bad enough that a rough Lake Superior had stranded the lifesavers, who would be there for four days.

Everyone stood on the beach and watched as Lake Superior pounded on the *Sitka*. The raging winds and waves swept away the deckhouses. Next, the rudder broke loose, and finally the *Sitka* broke in two. In just a couple days, Lake Superior had destroyed the *Sitka*. It lies on the shore, still easily seen scattered along the beach at Au Sable.

The light keepers had their hands full with the lifesavers there. They served forty meals to Trudell's men. Otto Bufe put in a request for reimbursement at twenty-five cents a meal. When the lifesaving crew left, they rowed to the *Sitka* and salvaged some of its navigation equipment, including compasses and sextant.

A few days later, Otto Bufe's pregnant wife became ill. He sent Assistant Sweet to Grand Marais to bring the local doctor. When he arrived, Mrs. Bufe was in a bad way. She gave birth to a baby boy, but the child was delivered stillborn. An entry in the log reads: "4 pm Mrs. Bufe was delivered of a dead male child." The following day, there was a funeral, and the infant was buried at the lighthouse.

The Bufes would lose another child the following year, and another grave was added at Au Sable. A month later, the Bufes were transferred to Point Iroquois near the Soo. Their tenure at Au Sable had been only two years, but it was full of tragedy and loss.

CHAPTER 6

MAJOR IMPROVEMENTS AND A MYSTERY

A s has been stated before, the only access to Au Sable Point Lighthouse was by boat. In 1905, however, a roadway was constructed that led to the lighthouse. Finally, occasional visits to Grand Marais to simply "get away" were now possible. Supplies would be easier to obtain as well. With the occasional crew of shipwreck victims or lifesavers dropping in, the food stores of the light keepers and their families were often devastated. Now they could go to town and restock. This was a major change for those living at Au Sable.

The road itself, a winding, sandy trail through the woods, was primitive and rough. The keepers frequently found the road impassable, especially in the spring and fall. The sand would often wash away, leaving deep ruts and washouts. Many supply trips were cut short due to the condition of the road.

If nothing else, getting away from the foghorn might have been necessary to save one's sanity. In 1905, the fog signal blew for 382 hours, the most ever recorded at the station. All the while it was blowing, men had to be near, shoveling coal and wood to keep the steam boilers hot. The sound of the monster horn blowing every few seconds would have been deafening and seemingly endless. Yes, even the wild frontier logging town of Grand Marais looked good after several days of the foghorn.

November 1905 brought a blizzard. It was one of those thick, wet and heavy early season snowstorms. A ship called the *Portage* was caught in the storm and was lost. It was off course and sailing blindly when it ran into Au Sable reef. Full of salt, it settled firmly in the rocks.

The Grand Marais lifesavers were called out, but the ship was stuck, not sinking. The lifesavers and the crew worked together and began shoveling salt over the side. The lifesavers were able to coax a few workers from Grand Marais to join in. All in all, they tossed seven hundred tons of salt into the water before the *Portage* eased itself off the reef.

When Otto Bufe and his wife left Au Sable, they were replaced by Thomas Irvine. Irvine helped with the wreck of the *Portage*. In the keeper's log, he wrote, "Steamer *Portage* up bound, ran on reef about ¾ mile N. of light at 9.25 P.M. 2ⁿᵈ Asst and myself rowed out and offered our assistance, sent 2ⁿᵈ Asst to Grand Marais with 2 seamen for tugs and life savers. I worked on her lightering salt." The following day, November 21, he wrote, "Steamer *Portage* still on reef. Tug *Westcott* with 25 laborers and life saving crew arrived at 10. A.M. to lighter her cargo. Capt. Trudell and Life Savers had dinner at station. Left here 4 P.M. to stand by steamer, still working on her at mid-night. Wind S & S.W. mod to strong at night and clear." Finally, on November 22, the efforts paid off: "Steamer *Portage* got off safely at 5:30 A.M. and went to Grand Marais. 2ⁿᵈ Asst. returned with provisions and mail." Things went back to their usual mundane routine around Au Sable.

Approximately three years later, something washed ashore at Au Sable. A man named Van Dusen spotted a small sailboat along the shore near the light station. The mast was broken, and it appeared to have been through some rough weather. He went up to the boat to get a closer look. Inside was the body of a dead man!

It looked like the body had taken a beating. The head had been beaten almost beyond recognition, and the shoulders and neck looked broken and battered. The dead man wore the uniform of the Lighthouse Service. Light Keeper Irvine recorded the incident: "2ⁿᵈ Asst ret. 9 A.M. Mr. Wm Van Dusen of Grand Marais reported a Light House boat ashore with a dead man in her about 9 mile W. of Station. I sent 1ˢᵗ Asst to report it to Life Saving Station. Crew arrived here 9 P.M. I went up with them and brought boat to station. They took body to Gd. Marais. Man apparently died from exposure, as he was lying under the forward deck, foremast gone, mainmast standing. Boat was in good shape, only one small hole in her. I think it is from Grand Island Light Station." The body was later identified as Assistant Keeper Edward Morrison from the north Grand Island Light Station. How he had come to Au Sable Point was a mystery. He was identified by a tattoo on his arm.

The body was taken back to Munising, and tales were coming in that the north Grand Island Light had been dark for a week. The idea that Morrison died from exposure faded quickly. A group of Munising residents went out to investigate. What they found only added to the mystery. The head light keeper, George Genery, had completely disappeared. The supplies he had brought back from Munising were still sitting on the dock. As the residents made a search of the light, they found nothing out of the ordinary. Genery's coat was hung on a hook in the boathouse. Morrison's vest was hanging on the back of a chair, and his watch was still in the pocket. Of the three boats that were normally left at the station, one source stated that one was missing while another source stated that two were missing. No one could understand what had happened.

The authorities began a search for the missing Genery, but he had completely disappeared. There were some who said they had seen Genery around the local bars in Munising drinking heavily, but none of these claims could be substantiated. Genery's wife, who was living in town, claimed she hadn't seen him either, but those who talked to her stated that she seemed unconcerned. The reason for this could be that Genery was reputed to have a temper and wasn't easy to work and/or live with. He had required a new assistant every season since his appointment, and his domestic life could have been just as rocky.

At the time, there were two basic theories as to what happened. The first theory is that the two men were murdered. The north point of Grand Island was another very isolated location. The lighthouse's nearest neighbor was the Grand Island gamekeeper, who lived seven miles away. When Genery and Morrison had been in town to pick up supplies, they had been paid. The pair was going back to the lighthouse with full pockets, and the north light would have been an ideal place for a robbery.

The second and more plausible theory is that Genery killed Morrison. The scenario goes as follows: Morrison brought the wheelbarrow down to the dock to help haul supplies back to the station. The evidence of this is the hung coat and vest, which would have meant that both men were in shirtsleeves, warm from the work. Because of Genery's personality and reputation, Morrison probably said something that set Genery off. In a flash of rage, Genery grabbed something like an oar or a shovel and beat in Morrison's skull. To hide the crime, he put Morrison in a boat and sent it out into Lake Superior, probably hoping it would never be found and that he could say his assistant had deserted. Or perhaps he was out in the boat and was hit with the boom from the sail. Whatever the case, Genery went into Munising and went on a several-day drinking binge. Afterward, he probably went home, and when news of the body found at Au Sable came in, he fled.

Strangely, before he died, Morrison sent a letter to his wife, who was living in Flint, Michigan. She received it four days after he had died. In the letter, he wrote, "Do not be surprised if you hear of my body being found dead along the shores of Lake Superior." He goes on to say that Genery was of a quarrelsome disposition and that he thought there might be an "accident" if he were to oppose him.

To this day, the mystery remains unsolved. No one really knows what happened to Morrison. Thomas Irvine, the light keeper who reported the discovery of the body, was transferred from Au Sable in 1908.

Irvine was eventually replaced by James Kay, who moved into the lighthouse with his family, keeping alive the tradition of packing people into the building like sardines. On visiting Au Sable that year, district lighthouse inspector James Smith came to the realization that living conditions at the light station were not good. It was cramped and unhealthy. It was time something was done about it. Inspector Smith proposed a reworking of the old building and the construction of a new one, a house that would be for the head keeper alone. The following spring, a work crew again arrived at the lighthouse.

It had been determined that the main dwelling would be reworked into a duplex. There had always been a separation of quarters for two families in the upper part of the building, but the main level had been an open community area. Now the structure would be divided into two separate dwellings, each with its own entrance.

During the construction, the families went about their daily routines. Even though it was difficult to work around the construction, it had to be heartening to see the changes and to know that in a few months, life at the station would be so much better. The families could be families again; they could have their privacy.

The new head keeper dwelling was built to match the old building. It had the signature red brick, the graduated peak on the roof and a porch that was given a roof on both dwellings. It became the Au Sable Point complex we know and see today.

It took all year to complete the head keeper's house. The top job would now have the perk of its own home. The head keeper position at Au Sable was now considerably better. Later that year, James Kay became the first keeper to move into the new building. He moved his family and his belongings across the walk into the freshly plastered house. It had to seem like such a relief—once again there was room, space.

With the living situation corrected at the station, the keepers could now feel like they were really going home when their daily routines were over.

They could spend more time with their families in a more private setting. It was an important and necessary change.

Ralph Tinkerham of the Department of Commerce's Lighthouse Establishment gives the following description of Au Sable in 1909: "The main point on which the lighthouse stands has been cleared of timber for a quarter mile each way from the station to facilitate the visibility of the light to the E[ast] and W[est]. This clearing has grown up to the second growth…small stuff. Access is by boat or wagon road to within three miles of the station, thence by foot trail; this trail is cleared out so that a team without a load can get to the light station."

Up until now, the federal government had always referred to Au Sable as Big Sable. On Lake Michigan, there was another lighthouse complex called Big Sable. When the French explorers first came to the New World, they made maps. The explorers tended to label things rather than name them. Examples include: Sault de Sainte Marie (Rapids of St. Mary), Grand Marais (Large Swamp or Marsh) and Aux Sable Pointe (Large Sand Point). The French terms are often repeated in their maps, with several locations receiving the same label. There are several Presque Isles around the Great Lakes and Michigan. In French, *presque isle* means "almost an island"—a place usually still attached to the shore by a small strip of land. Later, the point was designated Grand Sable Point and eventually became Big Sable Point. Having two places named Big Sable was confusing to the Lighthouse Service and the government when it came time for appropriations, so to end the confusion, Big Sable Point became Au Sable Point in 1910. The log reads, "Received letter from Inspector to day, changing name of station to Au Sable."

CHAPTER 7

MORE SHIPWRECKS

The forests around Au Sable Point continued to grow quieter. The logging crews for the Alger Smith Company had nearly clear-cut all the white pine in the region, and the company decided it was time to move on to the un-harvested regions around Duluth, Minnesota.

Approximately twelve miles away at Grand Marais, the population was decreasing as quickly as it had increased years before, as most of the loggers followed Alger Smith. In 1910, it was announced that the Manistique Railroad, which ran between Grand Marais and Seney, the town's main connection with the outside world, would no longer be making the run. Not only would the train stop, but the tracks were going with it as well. The company was leaving nothing behind. On November 5, 1910, the railroad made its last run to Grand Marais, essentially killing the town. Overnight, the population dropped from thousands to just two hundred. The people who were left were now cut off from the outside world, as, once again, the only way in and out was by ship.

This impacted Au Sable Point as well. Though the station residents still depended on the lighthouse tender to bring them supplies and restock the light, Grand Marais was their source for food stock. Grand Marais and those at the light station were once again dependent on supplies that might or might not make it past the "Shipwreck Coast."

It was a foggy July day in 1910 when the *Zenith City* was sailing along the Pictured Rocks shoreline, having left Marquette several hours earlier. Loaded with iron ore, the steel-hulled freighter was shipping under a good head of steam when it ran into the reef about a mile offshore. Fortunately, the ship wasn't in very bad shape, so it was pulled off the rocks without too much trouble. Several of its bottom plates would have to be repaired.

In the earlier years of Au Sable Point, most of the ships sailing by were of wood construction. With the rise of the Industrial Revolution and the need for bigger and stronger ships on the Great Lakes, steel construction ore freighters came into being. The demand for iron ore was growing by leaps and bounds, though the copper boom had played out, leaving ghost town after ghost town in the Keweenaw. Construction of new and larger ships shifted into high gear. As the wooden ships failed more and more either from age or shipwrecks, they were quickly being replaced by ships that were bigger, better and stronger.

The *Zenith City* was the largest freighter of its kind at the time. At 388 feet, it was the great ancestor of the 1,000-footers we see today. Even the ships' design remains unchanged. If it weren't for its steel construction, the *Zenith City* would never have left Au Sable reef to sail another day.

Farther out in Lake Superior, other tragedies were happening—tragedies discovered only when the ships were overdue, their fates unknown. Evidence of this washed up on the shore at Au Sable in the form of a grim message in a bottle in 1910. The log entry leaves us with a mystery: "2nd L. Mosen of Grand Marais found a bottle with a slip of paper containing the following: Lake Superior Aug 4th 1901. To those who finds this. Gone down with all hands. Steamer *Mappleton*. Lord have mercy on us all. Capt. Stinson." The bottle had been floating in Lake Superior for nine years. Maybe now those who had been waiting for the long-overdue ship would know it had been lost.

In searching records, there seems to be no evidence of a steamer named *Mappleton*. There are a few Captain Stinsons on record, but since the note doesn't include a first name or initial, locating the right one is problematic. Captain Stinson, the *Mappleton*, its crew and their fate seem to be lost in time.

In 1909, a captain from Grand Marais by the name of Ora Endress purchased a small wooden steamer called the *South Shore*. With the railroad gone from Grand Marais, a vital link had been taken away from those who remained in the community. Something had to be done to fill that void. Endress's idea was to make regular supply runs along the south shore of Lake Superior from Whitefish Bay to Marquette. The upper deck of the ship held cabins, allowing Endress to book passengers as well. He scheduled the *South Shore* to make stops at places like Whitefish Point, Vermillion, the Two-

Hearted River, Grand Marais and Au Sable. The *South Shore* was a regular sight on the lake and an occasional visitor to Au Sable, dropping off supplies or personnel for the light station.

Endress did quite well with his business until late November 1912. November is never a good time to have to sail the Great Lakes. The unpredictability and the utter and complete violence of the gales have taken hundreds of ships to the bottom. And hurricane-force winds and blizzards can—and often do—come with these November storms. Endress was sailing the *South Shore* toward Grand Marais from Sault Ste. Marie when the ship became engulfed in a blinding snow. A northeast gale had blown up, and things were getting dicey fast. The waves had built, and it became apparent that the *South Shore* wouldn't be able to get into Grand Marais harbor.

Endress had spent many years on the Great Lakes. He was well seasoned and knowledgeable, but now he had to make a difficult decision. With four passengers and ten crewmen on the ship, Endress chose the option he thought would give the ship and those on board their best chances of survival. He decided to try to ride out the storm in the open water. He put the bow to the wind and hoped for the best.

The storm blew mercilessly into the night. But Endress, keeping his bow to the waves, was working his way northeast out into Lake Superior. He had sailed almost halfway to Caribou Island, about twenty-five miles out from Grand Marais. The waves were beating against the ship and rolling over the decks. Slowly, the ship's seams started to open. A huge wave came and swept away part of the cabin house. Another wave pounded in part of the wheelhouse. The raging surf broke out windows and covered the *South Shore* in a sheet of ice. Water coming in the hull reached the boiler fires and extinguished them. The *South Shore* was without power.

The helpless ship was driven before the storm. It rose and fell between the massive troughs of waves. The wet and cold passengers and crew all manned the hand pumps, trying to keep the beleaguered ship afloat. It was a long night, but as morning rolled around, the ship was still afloat.

In the morning, the Grand Marais lifesavers spotted the *South Shore* about ten miles out. Endress, who was likely too busy trying to save his ship, wasn't flying any distress flags. But Captain Trudell deduced that they might need help, and there just might have been a small desire to take out the station's new motor-powered surfboat, named the *Audacity*. The days of rowing were behind the lifesavers—at least as long as the motor didn't conk out. Motorized surfboats made the Life-Saving Service more efficient. They were quicker to respond to wrecks and quicker to unload passengers and crew. It had been a major improvement for the lifesavers and those who depended on them.

When they reached the *South Shore*, the ship was nearly awash and foundering, as it was very full of water. They tried everything. They jettisoned the cargo and helped work the pumps. At one point, they even tried to rebuild the boiler fire, but it was to no avail. A decision had to be made. The lifesavers took off the four passengers and the ten crewmen and headed back to shore.

The abandoned *South Shore* was now at the mercy of Lake Superior. It was blown west toward Au Sable Point and Grand Sable Dunes. All the while, Lake Superior continued to batter the ship. Eventually, it rolled toward the shore and sank in twelve feet of water. The *South Shore*'s final resting place would be the location where Au Sable Point meets Grand Sable Dunes, west of the Devil's Log Slide.

The loss of the *South Shore* caused considerable hardship, as it was carrying the winter stockpile for many along the route. The winter was lean for those waiting for the *South Shore* to make its run, a run it never completed.

The *South Shore* can sometimes still be seen. It's quite visible when standing atop the log slide and gazing across the vastness of Au Sable Point, the lighthouse in the distance. When you look down at Lake Superior, look below the log slide but toward Au Sable. The shape of the *South Shore* can be seen under the shallow water. From time to time, the sand will cover and uncover the remains of the ship. So, like the ghost it is, the *South Shore* appears only occasionally, when the conditions are just right.

Improvements in technology were always slow to arrive at the Au Sable light station. In 1913, a new system for lighting the beacon was finally installed. As part of a nationwide upgrade to light beacons, the new oil-vapor system would increase the beacon's output ten-fold. The new technology was so efficient that the output of the light would increase from 1,200 candlepower to 28,000, allowing it to be seen an incredible nineteen miles out.

But that didn't help the ship *Wyoming*. Actually, nothing could help the *Wyoming*. October 1914 brought with it the usual gales, and a northwester hit when the *Wyoming* was passing Au Sable Point. As it attempted to turn and run before the storm, likely an effort to dash into Grand Marais harbor, the *Wyoming* fell deep into a trough of waves. The ship struggled desperately to get itself back on course, but the main straps that held the hull together blew apart, and the fastenings broke. The ship opened up at

Au Sable Point Lighthouse, 1912. Two of the light keepers can be seen on the porch, while the additional keeper's residence can be seen in the background. *Courtesy of the National Park Service.*

the top deck and amidships. The *Wyoming* was done. The crew was picked up by the lifesavers. Miraculously, no lives were lost.

In 1915, during World War I, it was decided that both the U.S. Life-Saving Service and the U.S. Revenue Cutter Service would become part of the U.S. Coast Guard. Congress had become somewhat border paranoid with the onset of the Great War. Spies and threats abounded, so the Great Lakes border with Canada seemed like a weak point in the country's homeland defense. Though the Coast Guard wasn't a military branch, it did have interdiction abilities and could stop, search and seize ships or men if something seemed suspicious. It would also simplify matters if all three entities were under the same umbrella. This change directly affected Benjamin Trudell and his lifesavers at Grand Marais. They had now become members of the Coast Guard and would have more funding to ensure that the station's needs were met. The biggest boon would be the upgrade in lifesaving boats.

Now Coast Guard lifesavers, the men at the Grand Marais station would be called to Au Sable on October 1, 1918. The *Gale Staples*, a wood-hulled steam freighter, was sailing toward Port Arthur with a full load of coal. It had left Sault Ste. Marie only a few hours earlier when a north gale blew up. The Lake Superior wind forced the *Gale Staples* onto the sandstone reef at Au Sable.

A lookout at the Grand Marais station saw the *Gale Staples* run aground. Trudell was away on a short leave, so his number-one surfman, Kristofferson,

The *Gale Staples*, one of the many victims of Au Sable reef, ran hard aground in October 1918. Efforts to free the ship were futile, and it remains there today. *Courtesy of the National Park Service.*

roused the men. They launched their newly motorized lifeboat and busted through the ever-worsening waves and wind.

Meanwhile, the ship had also been sighted by the light keepers at Au Sable. A log entry reads, "Steamer *Gale Staples* of Port Arthur Canada coal laden grounded on the reef about half or three quarters of a mile North West by North in plain sight of the station. 1st and 2nd assistants went out to see if they could render any assistance."

The steamer didn't seem to be in bad shape, so Kristofferson and his men returned to Grand Marais, leaving the crew behind. When they returned, they sent telegrams to the Soo calling for tugs to help and to get advice from the ship's owners. Later, the Coast Guard crew returned to the *Gale Staples* and watched over the ship for the night.

The following day, they returned to Grand Marais, bringing with them one of the sailors and two female cooks. They were all given a hot dinner when they arrived at the station. They later returned to the ship and came back with four more crewmen. The captain of the *Gale Staples* sent them with word that all of the crewmen who were ashore should be put up in hotels there at Grand Marais.

Again, the Coast Guard crew went back to the steamer. This time, the wind had picked up, and the waves were breaking over the deck of the ship. The surf was getting bad, with larger and larger rollers slamming the stranded ship's broadsides. There was a growing danger that the *Gale Staples* could break up. The captain made the decision to abandon ship and had the Coast Guard crew take everyone to shore.

Another entry in the Au Sable log shows that the proceedings were being watched by the keepers: "Coast Guards from Grand Marais took off the crew of the stranded steamer at 5 P.M. One of the yawl boats broke away and washed ashore east of the station. Keepers had a hard time to save it from being pounded to pieces among the rocks."

The following day, Lake Superior quieted. The *Gale Staples* was still intact, but the reef was beginning to grind away at the hull. The captain and ten of his men returned to the ship. In the meantime, Trudell had returned to the station and took over the rescue operations. His years of service in Grand Marais had led him to understand the moods of Lake Superior, and he knew the treacherousness of the waters. He suspected things might change. He cancelled all leave for any of his men and set them to work getting their rescue equipment ready just in case.

For three days, the weather was reasonable. Trudell and his men were spending their time taking telegrams to and from the stranded ship. Request after request was sent for tugs and a lighter ship to lift the cargo off and salvage what they could. They were assured that help was on the way.

At Au Sable, the keepers were watching the drama being played out in front of the lighthouse. The *Gale Staples* was being worn to pieces by the waves. A comment in the lighthouse log reads, "General Duties. Steamer's upper cabin is gone. Appears to have broken in two forward of the cabin." The *Gale Staples* was now in increasingly bad shape.

The next day, the tug and lighter finally arrived. Trudell and his men guided the tug carefully through the sandstone outcrops of the reef, leading it safely to what was beginning to look like the newest addition to Au Sable's collection of wrecks. On that same trip came an insurance inspector for the owners of the *Gale Staples*. He wanted to assess the situation himself, and he wasted no time in declaring the ship an unsalvageable wreck. The cargo was removed, and the *Gale Staples* was condemned to death by waves.

The keepers had been following the drama being played out in front of the light station: "Tug and lighter arrived at the wrecked steamer at 10 A.M. and commenced removing her cargo. Left for the harbor at 5 P.M." A log entry the following day read, "Tug and lighter abandoned *Staples* at 6 P.M. and proceeded up the lake."

Lake Superior wasted no time in battering the *Gale Staples* to pieces. To this day, remains of the ship surround the lighthouse on both sides. One of the last log entries about the *Gale Staples* confirms the ship's fate: "Blowing gale seas running over wrecked steamer moving her shore word [*sic*]." Pieces of the ship's hull are scattered amongst those of the *Sitka* to the west, and other pieces lie alone on the sandstone a few hundred yards to the east. The bottom of Lake Superior surrounding the point has uncounted pieces of the *Gale Staples* that can be seen below the surface in the amazingly clear water when boating or diving the reef.

Au Sable Point remained quiet for a time. The daily routines went on. The grounds always had to be kept up, as did the residences. There were repairs, and the buildings were painted annually, as the wear of the Lake Superior weather continued to take its toll. Gardens were dug to supplement the food supplies, though growing in sand can be a challenge. Some of the keepers brought in their own dirt. Educational materials for the children of the families staying at the light station were a part of the rotating library.

U.S. Lighthouse Service inspectors would come and go, and the wives of the keepers were held to the strict standards of keeping up the lighthouse.

Wreckage of the *Gale Staples*. Shipwrecks along the shore at Au Sable were plentiful and today serve as attractions at the national park. *Courtesy of the National Park Service.*

Occasionally, the inspector would create some competition between the couples. He would take a light keeper aside and tell him that he was doing a good job but that his wife wasn't holding up her end. Later, the inspector would pull the wife aside and tell her that she was doing a good job but that her husband was slacking and needed to step it up a bit. The couple would then push each other to do their jobs better. If a light station was consistently unkempt, it could mean the offending keeper's career. The inspectors were known for their intense "white glove" inspections.

On many occasions, there were visitors to the lighthouse, and the head keeper would entertain while the assistants went on with the station duties. Dozens of log entries mention visitors from Grand Marais, Grand Island, Munising and even places like Chicago and Detroit.

In Grand Marais in 1923, a major change took place that would affect all those around, including Au Sable Point. Benjamin Trudell retired. Trudell had demanded the very best of his men, and he had held the station to the highest standards since the moment it opened. To this day, Trudell is considered a legend of the U.S. Life-Saving Service. His shoes would be hard to fill.

One of the many families who helped man the station taking a portrait on the big porch.
Courtesy of the National Park Service.

After retirement, Trudell made an interesting admission. It was something he'd rarely told anyone while he was in active service, but now that he was retired, he was ready to admit it: "If there ever is any event of importance happening, I dream about it in advance. I always have. My mother was the same way. She told me I would be gifted with unusual things. Anything important in my work, in my business, I dream of. And when it happens the next morning, I remember it. It's not exactly the same, you know, but the conditions are similar." As an example, he revealed the following story:

During my second year in the Life-Saving Service, in 1892, I was stationed at Deer Park [a few miles east of Grand Marais]. *I was called to go on watch at 12 o'clock midnight, so I went to bed and slept from eight till twelve, and the dream happened at the very time a sinking was going on.*

I dreamed that I met a man on the beach, coming towards me. He appeared to be an acquaintance, yet I was doubtful as he got nearer. He was very nicely, finely dressed. As I approached him, he held out his hand to shake hands, but his hand was cold and clammy and I couldn't hold the grasp. Then he turned and walked towards the water and dissolved in the surf.

I was awakened standing in the middle of the dormitory, wet with perspiration. The relief watch was holding a lighted lantern to my face, asking, "What is the matter?"

That morning at the breakfast table, seven of us were messing together, and I recited the dream to them. They laughed at me, but I said, "Watch out." As the day wore on and nothing happened, they all began to make fun of me, even the captain.

It was blowing a three-day gale, with high seas from the northwest. About two o'clock that afternoon a man stumbled into the station, stating he had been on a wreck and had been washed ashore, the only survivor. Not knowing the direction of any town, he followed along the beach until he arrived at the Deer Park Life-Saving Station. I was called to take the beach patrol west and I was the first one ashore. There was the body of a man lying on his face, stretched out. He was finely dressed, and appeared to be an aristocrat. As we rolled him over, his hand flipped over and struck mine. And I saw he was the man from my dream. The resemblance was very noticeable. He had a mustache, but no chin whiskers. His clothes were not wet in the dream, though. He was Peter C. Minch, millionaire owner of the Western Reserve, *the first steel ship to go down in the lakes.*

Ironically, the *Western Reserve* was the flagship of Minch's fleet. He had wanted to show it off to his family and sailed into Lake Superior against the advice of other mariners in Sault Ste. Marie. Believing his ship was stronger and better than all the rest, he sailed right into the storm. But he was wrong, and all aboard paid the price of his arrogance—all except wheelman Harry Stewart, the lone survivor who came stumbling into the lifesaving station. Stewart was Trudell's cousin!

In 1923, a new head keeper, Klass L. Hamringa, came to Au Sable Point. Hamringa, who had been in the Lighthouse Service for many years, had become a hero when he was instrumental in saving forty-one people from freezing to death on Isle Royale after the wreck of the *Monarch*. He found survivors who had been clinging to life in a makeshift shelter of brush and broken timber after the onset of a late season blizzard. They were cold and well on their way to freezing to death when Hamringa found them. He was able to get a message to a rescue ship, and they were all picked up. He received a commendation for his valorous conduct. Prior to that, Hamringa himself had been shipwrecked twice, so he understood the hardships and trials of surviving a shipwreck.

Hamringa's years as light keeper were relatively uneventful. There were no major wrecks, as ships were now being built to take on the rough seas. There were now more steel-constructed ships on the Great Lakes, most of the wooden vessels having sunk or retired as they became slow and inefficient. Any companies that could afford to replace wooden ships did, which was cutting down on the losses of both ships and lives. With fewer losses, there were higher profits. After World War I, steel ship construction reached an all-time high. Iron was in high demand. Losses during the war had caused a rebuilding of not only the naval power of the United States but also the shipping freighters. A frequent target of the war, there had been considerable losses of commercial transport ships. The reconstruction of the shipping fleet was a priority.

Au Sable's environment still created dangerous moments but on a smaller scale. In one log entry, Hamringa wrote, "Polishing whistles and cleaning in tower, fisherman from Grand Marais, windbound at station. Had to pull his boat up on boatway. Blowing hard from west." The next day, he added, "Fisherman left for Grand Marais this morning. Had to walk and leave boat at station [but is] glad for saving the boat and nets. Blowing gale." Hamringa had a bit of a sense of humor as well, as evidenced by an entry on August 27, 1928: "Working in yard. A porcupine visited station. (Didn't invite him back.)"

Au Sable Point Lighthouse with two of the light keepers on the porch, circa 1920. *Courtesy of Superior View Studio.*

For Hamringa, all was quiet and routine at Au Sable until his last year, 1929.

It was a season of storms and shipwrecks. In August, a tug named the *Barrallton* was towing a 313-foot barge named *Lake Frugality*. They were heading toward Au Sable and Sault Ste. Marie when they were hit by a storm from out of the northeast. The tug was heading into the face of it, and the waves were building. Suddenly, the cable snapped, leaving the *Lake Frugality* floating free and at the mercy of the rising seas. Fortunately, the ship didn't sink but instead grounded ashore along the beach west of the lighthouse.

The tug proceeded on until it got on the lee side of Whitefish Point. With a northeast blow, it would never have been able to get into Grand Marais harbor for refuge.

The Coast Guard arrived at the stranded ship. Seeing that it wasn't in peril of sinking, the small crew was left aboard. Three days later, the *Barrallton* made it back with the help of the Coast Guard.

At the end of August, another storm blew up. The *Alice L.*, a gasoline fishing tug, had gotten caught in a fast storm just east of Au Sable. Few details are known about the wreck, but when the *Alice L.* sank, it took someone with it. The icy cold of Superior had claimed another soul.

Keeper Hamringa's tenure was almost through. He was going to retire and tell stories to his grandchildren. Little did he know, however, that there were more stories to be made.

On November 29, 1929, a storm moved in from the north and rapidly turned into a blizzard. Steaming toward Au Sable was a freighter named the *Kiowa*, a sister ship to the *Lake Frugality*, which had run ashore a couple months earlier. The *Kiowa*'s holds were full of flaxseed headed for Chicago. The blizzard caught up with the ship and then engulfed it. The ever-growing seas were rough, and they tossed the steamer helplessly. Suddenly, the entire cargo of seed shifted to one side, causing the *Kiowa* to list terribly. It was so bad that water was coming in the portholes.

Captain Alex T. Young was terrified and ordered nine of his men into one of the lifeboats. He then got in the boat himself and ordered it to be lowered, leaving behind twenty-three of his men to fend for themselves. The ship was encased in a sheet of ice, and water was freezing everything, including the men. Young's men were lowering the lifeboat when one of the lines snapped, dumping them into Lake Superior. Cold and wet, six of the men were pulled back on board by their shipmates. Another managed to reach the lifeboat. The rest, including the captain, disappeared beneath the icy waves of Lake Superior.

The *Kiowa* drifted along the shore, pulled by the storm. Arthur Kronk, the first mate, was now the acting captain. The crew was afraid, and Kronk tried to keep them calm as the situation worsened. Things weren't looking good for the crew. But on shore, someone saw the *Kiowa*'s situation. Keeper Klass Hamringa wrote of the wreck in his personal journal:

On November 30, 1929, steamer Kiowa *drifted 6 miles west of the light station, with a northwest gale. The crew launched a lifeboat,* Saturday, *which capsized, drowning five of the men. Everything on board the* Kiowa *was coated with ice, making it impossible to launch the boats. The steamer was on the side, stern down, with a 45-degree list. Mr. Chilson and two others were coming from a hunting trip west of the light station at 2 pm Sunday in a small gas boat, with rowboat in tow. Seeing the steamer, they picked off three men and made for the lighthouse, as the wind began to pick up from the northeast. The men were almost frozen.*

We immediately sounded the whistle at 2 pm and gave danger signals for an hour or so. We could not see help coming, so we launched our gas boat. We started about dusk, and it was dark when we arrived at the steamer Kiowa. *Six men were accommodated in the gas boat—5 in the rowboat, and 5 in Chilson's boat. When we had the crew all off and were about a mile from the boat, following the shore line, making for a hunting camp about 4 miles from the station, we saw the light of the Coast Guard boat coming. Flashing them signals, we ran alongside and put 16 of the crew on the Coast Guard boat, which took them to Grand Marais.*

After the retirement of Benjamin Trudell, the Coast Guard station at Grand Marais wasn't as efficient as it had been in the past. The men had extra duties added to their routines as they became more and more assimilated into the Coast Guard. Therefore, when Au Sable signaled for aid for the *Kiowa*, the Coast Guard did not respond as quickly as it might have in the past. The crews had been working on a submarine telephone cable when the Au Sable whistle blew. Coast Guard reports state that the men dropped the repair job and responded to the distress call promptly. However, Keeper Hamringa's journal doesn't bear that out—nor does his entry in the light station log: "Sunday about 2 P.M. a boat came to station telling us that a boat got ashore last night, some time between 7–8 P.M. Weather clear at the time. 5 men lost their lives. Started to sound signal for Coast Guard at 2 P.M. Did not come till dark. Sent 1st asst in station gas boat and row boat and the hunting party in their gas boat. Got the crew of 15 men before the Coast Guard hove in sight."

Supposedly, the Coast Guardsmen scrambled to the lifeboat and headed for the light station at Au Sable. But why did they not appear until after dark? Going overland was impossible, as the blizzard had now deposited heavy, wet snow into huge drifts. They claim they stopped at the Au Sable Point Lighthouse and learned from the keeper that the *Kiowa* was on the shore west of Au Sable.

If the Coast Guard spoke with anyone, it would have been one of the keepers' wives. The two assistant keepers had accompanied Hamringa to assist with their own rescue after Chilson had deposited the first load of the *Kiowa* crew, and they had already removed a second load of the crew before they encountered the Coast Guard.

The Coast Guard log regarding the incident is detailed in all aspects except in how they removed the crew from the *Kiowa*. It gives the impression that the Coast Guard rescued all of the *Kiowa*'s crew, stating, "removed all 16 of the remaining crew safely." It says nothing about the part played by Chilson, his hunting buddies and the light keepers in saving what was left of the crew.

Three days after the wreck of the *Kiowa*, a Grand Marais fishing tug, the *Josephine Addison*, saw a lifeboat floating in the water. It was the lifeboat from the *Kiowa*. The one crewman who had managed to climb aboard was still on it. He was encased in ice, the sixth fatality of the *Kiowa*.

The crew members who had been dropped off at the lighthouse were still there. The Coast Guard didn't return for them immediately because they had to make a run out to another steamer in trouble, the *George H. Donovan*. They piloted the ship into the harbor to safety. It was another day before they could get back to Au Sable to pick up the rest of the crew. Chilson and his two hunting partners were still there as well, and they went back to Grand Marais. In the bad weather, the harbor had frozen, and they had to break the ice to get back into the bay.

The *Kiowa* was one of the worst wrecks in the area, and shipwreck historians have debated whether the Grand Marais Coast Guard had "missed" the rescue and tried to "gloss" over the mistake with the report.

Light Keeper Hamringa and his two assistants, John R. Hamann and William Campbell, received commendations for the assistance they lent to the crew of the *Kiowa*. If it weren't for them and, of course, Chilson and his hunting partners, the unsung heroes of the rescue, the loss of life would have been much higher. Hamringa had again come through for those in distress. He retired two weeks later after a lifetime of distinguished service and another commendation from the Lighthouse Service. Heroes shine when heroes are needed.

And with this incredible flurry of death and destruction, Au Sable became quiet again.

CHAPTER 8

THE SUNSET YEARS

T he sailing ships were gone. The age of steel and the diesel freighter had taken over. Postwar shipbuilding efforts had put new and stronger ships on the Great Lakes. Fleets of big, steel ore haulers now plied the waters, visible on the distant horizon. Shipbuilders were turning out ships that were more seaworthy, as well as keeping in mind World War I. If the United States were ever to enter a conflict similar to the "war to end all wars," the ships would need to be able to be used for an emergency war effort. A constant supply of iron would be crucial to any future war effort. Additionally, the Soo Locks could be a target for sabotage. The army base there was in a constant state of preparedness, with daily drills from dawn until dusk. Ships needed to be able to make it through, and accidental sinkings had to become a thing of the past. Ships had to be better. And they were.

Of course, this didn't completely end maritime accidents on the Great Lakes. But as the years wore on, maritime tragedies became fewer and fewer. The practice of "coasting" had disappeared with the emergence of new technology such as radios and two-way communication. Now ships could keep in contact and warn each other of dangerous weather. Communication with the Coast Guard stations was also possible, giving ships and their captains the ability to radio for help. No longer were ships dependent on the aid of Coast Guard spotters.

The shipping routes worked their way farther out into Lake Superior, giving the Au Sable Point region a wide berth. The sandstone reef that had caused so much havoc over the years was now becoming simply a point of navigation on the route to and from the great iron ranges of Minnesota and Michigan. Though the lighthouse would still be important, its role in the past as a haven for the cold and shipwrecked, the lost and dying, was becoming less necessary. Its primary role now was to be a light on the horizon, informing sailors of their proximity to Whitefish Point and the safety of Whitefish Bay.

By the very nature of its location, Au Sable was usually late to catch up with the rest of the world. Conveniences that were becoming commonplace in homes elsewhere were slow to reach the light station. However, much of that changed in 1930. That year would see the arrival of a new head keeper, Arthur Taylor, as well as more work being done on the head keeper's dwelling and the assistant's building. The structures were about to be "modernized," including indoor plumbing. No longer were the private moments of life spent in a freezing, smelly outhouse. A gas cookstove was also added.

Thomas Edison's electric light also reached Au Sable Point Lighthouse that year, powered by a newly installed generator. Another big improvement was the addition of central heating, bringing much-needed warmth to the lighthouse. Last but not least, the world came to Au Sable when a radio was placed at the station. The sense of isolation moved a little further away.

Life was routine as always. The lighthouse logs give a feel for daily life in 1930:

> *Monday, August 4—Cleaning engine in signal. Mr. Campbell and Sons of Grand Marais at this station over night.*
>
> *Tuesday, August 12—Cleaning vapor light, cutting grass and weeds around station.*
>
> *Thursday, August 21—Repairing after deck of motorboat.* Amaranth *arrived 10 pm with coal.*
>
> *Friday, August 29—Too much sea to work on sea wall. Give lens and tower general cleaning.*

Life at Au Sable, as it had always been, was about keeping the light shining. Weekly runs to Grand Marais for supplies kept either the keeper or an assistant away for most of the day. Those trips had to be a nice break from the routines.

The 1931 logs record the process of getting the lighthouse into shape:

A circa 1931 photograph of the Au Sable Point boat dock, where all supplies were brought into this isolated place. *Courtesy of the National Park Service.*

April 10—Found Station in good condition. Put station in commission, same day.

April 11—Cutting ice off dock to get in water pipe.

April 12—Putting up rain trough and repairing rail.

April 13—Burning old grass and cleaning up grounds.

April 14—Fill cisterns in keeper's quarters and signal. Oliver Shelly, 2nd asst. arrived at station 10 am and reported for duty.

April 15—Cleaning and painting bottom of motorboat. Blasting ice off dock.

April 16—Fitting out motorboat.

April 16—Varnishing in keeper's quarters, cleaning in tower. Stannard Rock visible this 10 pm.

These chores continued on well into May. The entire complex had to be painted. There was constant upkeep on the dock, which was endlessly battered by the force of Lake Superior's waves. Trees and gardens were also planted.

But there were still days like July 10: "Mr. Barney of Grand Marais arrived at station 12 am asking me if I would call the Coast Guard, as his motor was toteley [*sic*] broken down. Coast Guard arrived 1 pm towing him into Grand Marais."

The keepers had to be jacks-of-all-trades during these years. Excerpts from the daily logs record things like "grinding valve on No. 2 engine," "pouring cement for new sidewalk" and "pipe to the diaphone broke, will have to get it rethreaded in Grand Marais." The keepers had to know how to do everything. They were plumbers, masons, electricians, carpenters, landscapers and painters all in one.

In October 1933, a tug and derrick barge were hit by a gale off Au Sable Point. The two ships were towing a string of pontoons carrying discharge pipe from a dredging operation. When the storm hit, the cable pulling the string of pontoons broke. The lighthouse log described the incident: "North west gale, Keeper going to Grand Marais and reporting to Coast Guard lots of wreckage pontoons coming ashore." The log for the following day reads, "Coast Guard helping tug to pick up floating pontoons, lots of them along the beach." The pontoons had scattered from Au Sable Point to Grand Marais, covering the shore along Grand Sable Dunes.

More small incidents like this would happen, but the years of big wrecks were over. Au Sable's threat had mellowed with age, and the ships no longer sailed close enough for the reef and Lake Superior to conspire against them.

In 1935, another marvel of modern technology that had eluded Au Sable station finally arrived. A telephone line was run to the lighthouse, and phone service was available for the first time.

In 1939, the world was again beginning to feel the threat of war. Franklin Delano Roosevelt was very conscious of the growing threat building up in Germany and Italy. Just before the onset of World War II, he placed the Lighthouse Service under control of the Coast Guard. Like years before, when the Life-Saving Service had been absorbed into the Coast Guard, so now was the Lighthouse Service.

With this change, the Coast Guard immediately modernized the quarters even more by wiring all the buildings for electricity and installing a diesel generator to run it all. The road was also upgraded, making things easier for traffic coming to and from the lighthouse. There was even a garage built for the keepers.

Reflected in the log entries was the fact that the keepers were now required to do beach patrol and other Coast Guard duties that hadn't previously been a part of their job: "November 13, 1940—Fresh south west wind, cloudy with light snow. 1st asst and 2nd asst went 4 miles west and 1 mile south looking for dead bodies of some Canada boat. Went down. Orders from Command Officer, patrol beach 4 mile north, 2 mile south from light, and fix boat room door."

During World War II, a revolutionary device was invented that would change the face of shipping on the Great Lakes: radar. This invention, which

A circa 1940 aerial view of Lake Superior. Notice the roads cut into the woods, finally giving automotive access to the light. *Courtesy of the National Park Service.*

An aerial view of the complete lighthouse complex, 1944. Even the great foghorn building can be seen in the foreground. This picture was taken during the winter, as evidenced by the ice buildup seen along the shore. Also note the waves breaking over part of the treacherous reef near the top. *Courtesy of the National Park Service.*

The sedan helps date this photo of Au Sable Lighthouse to the 1940s. *Courtesy of Superior View Studio.*

The lighthouse complex surrounded by vintage vehicles. This photo was taken in 1945 after a road had finally reached Au Sable. *Courtesy of Superior View Studio.*

was created as an early warning system to spot enemy aircraft, also had the ability to show intense storm fronts on its screen. It could also show the landscape through fog and darkness. Ships would no longer be lost or caught off guard by a storm front.

Under the Coast Guard, keepers at Au Sable were turned over quickly. Most lasted only a season and the rest a mere two years. Between 1945 and 1958, there was only one keeper who lasted longer: Toivi W. Linnamaki. He served seven of those years. There were six different keepers in thirteen years.

In the 1950s, the Coast Guard deemed that it was no longer necessary to man the lighthouses and began automating them. An era of American history was coming to an end. Lighthouse complexes along all the coasts became unmanned and abandoned, left to the elements. The Coast Guard issued the following statement: "The lighthouse keeper gave a reliability critical to equipment of his time. It was equipment susceptible to failure and needed constant attention. Technology has changed. We no longer need a man there 24 hours a day with an oil can."

Though the Coast Guard's statement is true, it misses the point of the keeper, who offers a hand and human compassion to those in distress. It misses the importance of hot food for those cold and frozen in the night. It misses heroes and brave men who would risk all to help their fellow man in need. It misses the heart of the lighthouse keeper and the debt that was owed to every last one.

In the case of the Au Sable Point Lighthouse, the automation announcement came from the Coast Guard on July 30, 1957. It read, "The chief difficulty with this unit is the fact that it is remotely located some 14 miles by road from Grand Marais. The road is a tortuous path over sand dunes and through wooded areas, frequently made impassable by snow and washouts.

Women played important and pivotal roles in life at lighthouses. *Courtesy of the National Park Service.*

Transportation of school age children via government vehicle over this road to the nearest school is unfair to the children."

With that, the last three Coast Guard keepers were reassigned to Grand Marais. They would be required to make periodic stops at Au Sable Point to ensure the automated light's continued operation. The Fresnel lens was disassembled and shipped to the district headquarters in Cleveland, Ohio. A special battery-powered bulb was installed as the new light. This reduced the intensity of Au Sable's beacon. The fog signal was removed, and the buildings were boarded up. No longer needed, the lighthouse would become another relic of past days of the Great Lakes, left to the mercies of Lake Superior and abandoned like the remains of the ships that surrounded it. Its future was uncertain.

CHAPTER 9

THE NATIONAL PARK SERVICE

I n 1961, the lighthouse acreage at Au Sable was declared excess property by the Coast Guard. The result of this was that the lighthouse and its buildings began to fall into disrepair. Abandoned buildings don't last long on the shore of Lake Superior. The harsh environment takes its toll quickly. Back in the early 1900s, a large portion of the land between Munising and Grand Marais had been purchased by lumbering companies during the logging boom. When the lumber boom played out, the properties were abandoned and reverted to the State of Michigan for back taxes. Virtually all the land between the two towns now belonged to the state. In order to do something about it, the state went to work with the federal government in an effort to recognize the natural wonders of the Pictured Rocks. If the federal government designated the region as a national park, the state's problem would be solved. Negotiations continued, and eventually the two reached an agreement.

Dominic Jacobetti, the Upper Peninsula's state representative at the time, passed a bill that enabled the land to be deeded to the federal government. In 1966, Congress authorized a bill that would establish the Pictured Rocks National Lakeshore, the first one of its kind in the United States. The bill stated that the National Lakeshore would be created "in order to preserve for the benefit, inspiration, education, recreational use, and enjoyment of the public, a significant portion of the diminishing shoreline of the United States and its related geographic and scientific features."

President Lyndon Johnson signed the bill, and Pictured Rocks National Lakeshore received the first National Lakeshore designation in the country. Its boundaries would cover the entire forty-two miles of shore between Munising and Grand Marais and encompass not only the Pictured Rocks cliff formations but also Grand Sable Dunes and points between. But not Au Sable Point.

The land at Au Sable had been turned over to the General Services Administration by the Coast Guard. Completely surrounded by parkland, Au Sable was isolated. The abandoned complex was deteriorating from the weather, with the smaller outbuildings suffering the most. Some of the main buildings had been broken into, and there had been some vandalism. Some of the trim and walnut stair railings had been used to fuel campfires. Windows were broken out, and window frames had been broken and burned. Sadly, Au Sable had become a home for varmints and a target for the curious, who poked through the abandoned buildings.

In 1968, the General Services Administration turned the property over to the Department of the Interior and the National Park Service. Au Sable was finally a part of the National Lakeshore. The park service was given the deed to the property and the buildings, though the Coast Guard retained the tower. Though now automated, the light at Au Sable was still in operation and was serviced by the Coast Guard regularly. The light was now mounted on the iron handrail of the gallery on the outside of the tower. For maintenance purposes, the Coast Guard still required access to the tower.

But was it too late to bring the lighthouse complex back to life? Had exposure to the weather and a decade of vandalism taken too much of a toll?

From the moment Au Sable Point Lighthouse complex became a part of the park, the National Park Service was intent on restoring it. The restoration was immediately incorporated into the future plans of the park.

Pictured Rocks National Lakeshore is a large park that contains many diverse areas of natural beauty. When the park came into being in 1966, all of those areas had to be catalogued, and decisions had to be made as to what areas would attract the most visitors. The main draw at Pictured Rocks had always been its natural wonders, and access to those would have to be first priority. Roads and trails would have to be created. Campgrounds would have to be located and designed in a way that didn't disrupt the natural beauty of the surroundings. Au Sable Point Lighthouse would have to wait.

After receiving the deed to the lighthouse complex, the park service went in and "stabilized" the structures. It sealed up the buildings to protect them from the wind and weather. As part of the park, Au Sable Point would see even more visitors, so for their own safety, as well as the safety of park patrons, the buildings were locked up and boarded tight. There they would stand, empty but watched over. The old complex would attract visitors and hikers, as would the remains of the old wrecks.

It wasn't until 1988, twenty years later, that the resources and time were forthcoming for Au Sable.

Pictured Rocks National Lakeshore had developed into a wonderful collection of natural wonders. There were waterfalls, beaches, rock formations and wilderness, all linked together with a complex system of hiking trails. But the one cultural resource contained within the park had yet to be mined. Au Sable Point and its lighthouse complex were rich in Great Lakes history. The national park was already using the Life-Saving Station at Grand Marais as its eastern headquarters, and the Sand Point station in Munising served as its western and main headquarters. Au Sable Point had been waiting patiently for its turn.

Around the Great Lakes, many of the historic lighthouse complexes had been left to the elements after being decommissioned. Their buildings fell into such disrepair that many were little more than ruins and weren't salvageable or restorable. Some were lost forever. A few had been sold off to private interests and were turned into small businesses or bed-and-breakfasts. The only way to view them would be a several-hundred-dollar overnight stay. Of course, many come equipped with their own special lighthouse ghost.

As it stood, Au Sable Point was still in restorable condition. Just as important was the fact that it was now one of the last complete lighthouse complexes still intact. The National Park Service's efforts at stabilizing the buildings had worked. Miraculously, that included the outbuildings like the oil storage shed and the fog signal building. Not only would Au Sable Point be able to represent itself as a part of Lake Superior history, but it would also stand as a representative of light stations throughout the Great Lakes. And it would be open to the public.

First, there was the research that had to be done. Professionals performed analysis of the plaster and paint, and the plans for the original structures were revisited. The wood in the trim and the balustrades of the stairs had to be matched. Even the style and shape of the shingles had to be uncovered. No detail was too small.

The buildings were measured in detail by a survey crew from the Historic American Buildings Survey, which produced highly detailed drawings of the station complex. It would take time, but at least things were moving in a positive direction.

Even the original sidewalks and walkways were restored. Shown here are workmen repairing part of the sidewalk that led to the foghorn building. *Courtesy of the National Park Service.*

All the buildings in the lighthouse complex had to be restored. Even the small outbuildings and storage sheds were meticulously brought back to life. *Courtesy of the National Park Service.*

Workers restoring the main lighthouse building. Surrounded by scaffolding, the old building gets a much-needed face-lift. *Courtesy of the National Park Service.*

Workmen rebuild the great porch, which had become dilapidated after the lighthouse was decommissioned, during restoration of the Au Sable Point complex. *Courtesy of the National Park Service.*

The restoration began with simple, basic things like getting some paint on the buildings. Though advances in maritime safety had rendered Au Sable Point a danger no longer, the annual Lake Superior storms and harsh weather continue annually. Like in days of old, painting Au Sable would be a regular affair.

The first building slated to be worked on was the original building, now the double assistants' quarters, attached to the light tower. It was decided to restore the building to its circa 1910 appearance. This decision was in keeping with the plan to eventually restore the head keeper's building to its former purpose and re-create the era when three keepers were on staff.

This was the logical choice for a starting point, as it would also include work on the light tower. It, too, had been neglected over the years. Even with the Coast Guard maintaining the light, the interior had been left to the ravages of time and moisture. In the early 1990s, the light tower was worked on extensively. First, the exterior of the lens room was repainted its traditional black color. Workers then went to work on restoring the lens room itself. Since the light had been mounted on the outside of the tower, the original lens mechanism had been dismantled when the Fresnel lens was removed. These magnificent pieces of copper and brass had to be restored and reassembled.

The following year, the interior of the tower was painted. The woodwork was re-varnished and brought back to life. The old light was getting back into shape. When the lens room was finished, replica linen curtains were hung. The sun beating through the tower windows can make for a hot experience on the coolest day. Lens rooms can get unbearably hot. In the meantime, the Fresnel lens from Au Sable was located in Cleveland, where it had been stored for safekeeping. While the lantern mechanism was being restored, the Fresnel lens was shipped to the Grand Marais Maritime Museum (housed in the old lifesaving station), where it went on temporary display. In 1996, the lens was returned to Au Sable Point Lighthouse, where it was reinstalled in the same spot it had occupied for so many years. It was home.

With the tower restored, restoration began in earnest on the assistant keepers' quarters. The building was missing much of its woodwork, and replacements would have to be crafted. Much of the woodwork had been crafted from hardwoods that were now difficult to find. None of it would be easy to replace.

Throughout the 1990s, the Au Sable Point Lighthouse station was brought back to life. The head keeper's quarters were found to be in better condition than was anticipated. The plans for this building were interesting.

Painting the outside of the light tower is much easier now than it was in the old days. In this photograph, a workman on a cherry picker repaints the tower during restoration. *Courtesy of the National Park Service.*

Left: Although it was difficult, the walnut stair railing in the assistant keepers' dwelling was completely restored. *Photo by Mikel B. Classen.*

Below: Pictured Rocks National Lakeshore is a haven for nature sports enthusiasts. In this photograph, a kayaker paddles past the wreckage of the *Gale Staples*. *Photo by Mikel B. Classen.*

The downstairs would be a visitors' center, while the upstairs would become quarters for volunteers who stayed to run the center. Once again, the station would have keepers.

Au Sable entered the new century with new life and purpose. It would now become a place of education and interpretation. The Coast Guard still maintains a light there. A plastic Fresnel lens now surrounds a solar-powered lamp, and it still sends out the beacon that mariners have relied on for so long. But now the tower fills with visitors looking out over the vast expanse of Lake Superior. Hiking trails lead to the light station complex, and primitive campsites for backpackers have been cleared near the lighthouse. Tour guides paint pictures of Au Sable's past for visitors to envision. Pictures are taken, and memories are made. A large campground at the Hurricane River provides an easy walk down the old access road to the lighthouse. Following the beach leads to the remains of the *Mary Jarecki*, the *Sitka* and the *Gale Staples*. Au Sable Point is no longer a lonely place.

But Au Sable Point is still Au Sable Point, and Lake Superior is still Lake Superior. Any moment can bring a change. The wind shifts, the waves build and danger strikes without warning.

The following excerpt was taken from the sailing journal of Jim Wooll, who went on a month-long cruise on Lake Superior in August 2000:

> *Lake Superior let us know that wind was available after a three-day absence. We left in light winds and found 14 knots from the west as we cleared the harbor. The wind had built to 22 knots by Au Sable Light, and it had backed some. The shore turns to the south a bit, so we had beam winds, which we sailed with the staysail alone. We beam reached as the seas built to better than six feet. Bobbie became seasick, and I was just barely able to avoid sickness. It was gray, and we had light rain. The section of coast east of Munising is a National Seashore, the Pictured Rocks. We had hoped to see and photograph the large sand dunes before Au Sable Point and the sculptured and colored sandstone cliffs during the rest of the trip. Conditions did not permit any photos, so we can do it on our next visit. We anchored in a protected bay, had hot soup and a nap. The winds laid down about 9:00 that evening.*

One thing that can be counted on at Au Sable Point is that eventually, there will be bad weather. It is never a matter of if, only when—and it

Pieces of ships are scattered all along the shore at Au Sable Point. These remnants of times past serve as reminders of the tragedies and disasters that plagued this area. *Photo by Mikel B. Classen.*

is best to be nowhere near Au Sable Point at that time. As the explorer Radisson prophetically said so many years before, Au Sable Point is "most dangerous when there is any storms." Au Sable Point was and remains a most dangerous place.

EPILOGUE

Over the last decade, Alger County, which is where Pictured Rocks National Lakeshore makes its home, has been paving county road H-58 section by section. This is the road that runs between Grand Marais and Munising and provides access to Pictured Rocks attractions. This road used to be sand based, providing a rough ride for visitors—especially those with larger vehicles. Many a time, I witnessed the look of abject terror in the eyes of an RV driver when passing him on this narrow, tortuous drive.

These conditions made getting to Au Sable and much of Pictured Rocks

 difficult, particularly on the east half of the park. Like most of its history, Au Sable has never been very easy to get to. Getting to major campgrounds like Twelve-Mile Beach and the

Au Sable Point Lighthouse today, fully restored. Though its role as a lighthouse has changed, Au Sable's mission of providing a beacon in the night to mariners still remains. *Photo by Mikel B. Classen.*

Present-day Au Sable Lighthouse, fully restored. Thousands of visitors make the mile-long trek along the path or the wreckage-covered shoreline to see the lighthouse. There are tours during the summer months. *Photo by Mikel B. Classen.*

Hurricane River was difficult, and vehicles were often damaged trying to get there. Though it took several years to complete, the paving of H-58 changed everything for visitors to the park, and especially Au Sable Point. Finally, after all these years, there's a blacktop road to the Hurricane River and the path to the lighthouse.

The National Park Service has instituted an annual Au Sable Day. Additionally, there are Au Sable Point Lighthouse podcasts that can be downloaded. The lighthouse is officially part of the cyber age.

Now that the physical restoration of the light station is complete, the park service is trying to refurnish the interior of the assistant keepers' residence and accepting donations of lighthouse antiques. For more information on Au Sable Point Lighthouse, contact the National Park Service in Munising, Michigan, or log on to the website at www.nps.gov/piro/.

LIST OF LIGHT KEEPERS AT AU SABLE POINT LIGHTHOUSE

Head Keepers

Casper Kuhn, 1874–76
Napoleon Beedon, 1876–79
Frederick W. Boesler Sr., 1879–84
Gus Gigandet, 1884–96
Herbert Weeks, 1897–1903
Otto Bufe, 1903–05
Thomas E. Irvine, 1905–10
James Kay, 1910–15
John Brooks, 1915–23
Klass L. Hamringa, 1920–30
Arthur Taylor, 1930–36
Edward T. McGregor, 1937–45
D.S. Barclay, 1945–46
Fred A. Harju, 1946–47
John Balma, 1947
Toivi W. Linnamaki, 1947–54
Richard E. Miller, 1954–56
A.S. Mako, 1956–58

Assistant Keepers (as best as can be determined)

First Assistant Paul Happold, 1875–76
First Assistant Mrs. Mary Beedon, 1876–79
First Assistant Frederick Boesler Jr., 1879–82
First Assistant George Zenker, 1884–86
First Assistant William Laviate, 1886–87
First Assistant George Wilson, 1887–90
First Assistant Sevellon Northrup, 1890–92
First Assistant Mrs. Mary Gigandet, 1892–97
First Assistant James Dooley, 1897
First Assistant Martin Nelson, 1897–98
First Assistant Henry Luxton, 1898–99
First Assistant Winfield Addison, 1899–1900
First Assistant John Keating, 1900–03
First Assistant Orrin Young, 1903–08
Second Assistant Garfield Sweet, 1904–07
Second Assistant Emil Kohnert, 1907–08
First Assistant Emil Kohnert, 1908–11
Second Assistant John Brooks, 1908–11
First Assistant John Brooks, 1911–15
Second Assistant H.M. Laramie, 1911–25
First Assistant John Hanann, 1923–30
Second Assistant William Campbell, 1925–30
First Assistant Frederick Hawkins, 1936–39
Second Assistant Edgar Parker, 1939

REFERENCES

Arbic, Bernie. *City of the Rapids: Sault Ste. Marie's Heritage*. Allegan Forest, MI: Priscilla Press, 2003.

Carter, James L. *Voyageur's Harbor: A History of the Grand Marais Country*. Marquette, MI: Pilot Press, 1977.

Clary, David A. *Au Sable Light Station, Pictured Rocks National Lakeshore: The Life of the Keepers as Reflected in Their Official Journals*. N.p.: National Park Service, 1975.

Dorson, Richard M. *Bloodstoppers and Bearwalkers: Folk Traditions of the Upper Peninsula*. Cambridge, MA: Harvard University Press, 1952.

Hatcher, Harlan. *A Century of Iron and Men*. New York: Bob Merrill Company, 1950.

Law, W.H. *Deeds of Valor by Heroes and Heroines of the Great Water World*. Detroit: Pohl Printing Company, 1911.

National Park Service. *Au Sable–Big Sable Lighthouse Logs, 1876–1940*. N.p.: National Park Service, n.d.

———. *A History of Service: The Origins of the U.S. Coast Guard*. N.p.: National Park Service, n.d.

Radisson, Pierre Esprit. *The Journal of the Fourth Voyage of Exploration*. Paris, 1672.

Records of the U.S. Coast Guard, Grand Marais Life-Saving Station Logs, 1900–1930. National Archives, Washington, D.C.

Records of the U.S. Lighthouse Service, 1860—1957. National Archives, Washington, D.C.

Schoolcraft, Henry Rowe. *Schoolcraft's Narrative Journal of Travels*. East Lansing: Michigan State University Press, 1992.

Stonehouse, Frederick. *Great Lakes Crime: Murder, Mayhem, Booze and Broads*. Gwinn, MI: Avery Color Studios, 2004.

————. *Lake Superior's Shipwreck Coast: A Survey of Maritime Accidents from Whitefish Bay's Point Iroquois to Grand Marais, Michigan*. Gwinn, MI: Avery Color Studios, 1985.

Stonehouse, Frederick, and Daniel R. Fountain. *Dangerous Coast: Pictured Rocks Shipwrecks*. Gwinn, MI: Avery Color Studios, 1997.

Symon, Charles. *Alger County: A Centennial History*. Munising, MI: Bayshore Press, 1985.

Western Historical Company. *History of the Upper Peninsula of Michigan*. Chicago: Western Historical Company, 1883.

Williams, Ralph D. *The Honorable Peter White: A Biographical Sketch of the Lake Superior Iron Country*. Cleveland, OH: Penton Publishing Company, 1907.

INDEX

INDEX

ABOUT THE AUTHOR

The author stands on a part of the wreckage of the *Mary Jarecki*, one of several wrecks still visible at Au Sable Point. *Photo by Mary L. Underwood.*

Mikel B. Classen has been writing about northern Michigan in newspapers and magazines for over thirty-five years, creating feature articles about the life and culture of Michigan's north country. He's written about history, travel, the outdoors and many other subjects. A journalist, historian, photographer and writer with a fascination of the world around him, he enjoys researching and writing about lost stories from the past.

Classen has a passion for history and makes his home in the oldest city in Michigan, historic Sault Ste. Marie. He is also a collector of out-of-print history books, historical photographs and prints of Upper Michigan. At Northern Michigan University, he studied English, history, journalism and photography. He lives with his wife, Mary L. Underwood, and his Labrador retriever, Grand Sable Dune.

To learn more about Mikel B. Classen, check out his website at www.mikelclassen.com.